LEE'S BODY GUARDS

LEE'S BODY GUARDS

THE 39TH BATTALION VIRGINIA CAVALRY

MICHAEL C. HARDY

THE
History
PRESS

Published by The History Press
Charleston, SC
www.historypress.net

Front cover: *(top, left to right)* The first company of Lee's Body Guard was organized for service under Major General Richard S. Ewell. *Library of Congress*; Robert E. Lee *(center)*, Walter Taylor *(right)* and G.W.C. Lee *(left)* in an image taken a few days after the surrender at Appomattox. *Library of Congress*; Major General Jubal Early took over command of the Second Corps after Richard Ewell's reassignment. *Library of Congress*; *(bottom)* Lee observing the battle of Fredericksburg. *Library of Congress.*

Back cover *(inset)*: Lieutenant General James Longstreet played a critical role in the battle of Gettysburg. *Library of Congress.*

First published 2019

Manufactured in the United States

ISBN 9781467141505

Library of Congress Control Number: 2019937046

Notice: The information in this book is true and complete to the best of our knowledge. It is offered without guarantee on the part of the author or The History Press. The author and The History Press disclaim all liability in connection with the use of this book.

CONTENTS

INTRODUCTION

In 1964, Clifford Dowdey wrote, "The Army of Northern Virginia fielded no mobile telegraph system, and messages from telegraph stations and intra-army messages were carried by the hard-bitten, reckless young men who served as couriers." Those "hard-bitten, reckless young men who served as couriers" have received scant attention in the historiography of the Civil War. They are nameless components essential to the running of a mighty military machine that slogged through four years of destruction.[1]

The Thirty-Ninth Battalion Virginia Cavalry, or Lee's Body Guard, was truly unique in the annals of Confederate military history. While recruited as a battalion of scouts, guides and couriers, Lee's Body Guard seems to have been more frequently utilized in delivering messages and less frequently in scouting and guiding. That is not to say that these men did not scout and guide, nor does it mean they were not involved in combat operations, but the time they spent engaged in their other duties pales in comparison to the amount of work they did as couriers. They were clerks, wagoneers and messengers and operated in more mundane roles throughout their service. Yet, their participation was vital to the overall conduct of the war.

My interest in Lee's Body Guard came years ago, as I was researching a history of the Branch-Lane brigade. While seeking information on staff officers, I stumbled across an obituary for Catlett C. Taliaferro that claimed that fifteen-year-old Taliaferro ran away from college at the start of the war and joined the Ninth Virginia Cavalry. Taliaferro was assigned to General Thomas J. "Stonewall" Jackson as a courier, following Jackson from the battle

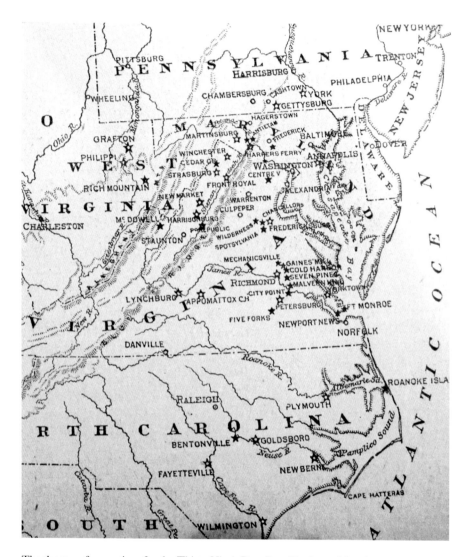

The theater of operations for the Thirty-Ninth Battalion. Battles and Leaders.

at Front Royal all the way to Lexington and, finally, witnessing Jackson's funeral. Then, Taliaferro was attached to General Robert E. Lee in the same role—as a courier. It was Taliaferro who rode with Lee to Appomattox and witnessed the surrender. Taliaferro's account—one that was passed down through his family—has some credibility issues. However, the story inspired me to dig more into the history of a largely forgotten battalion that had daily access to the Confederate high command.[2]

Previous research into this battalion and the role it played has been slight. J. Boone Bartholomees Jr. briefly mentions the role of couriers in his book *Buff Facings and Gilt Buttons: Staff and Headquarters Operations in the Army of Northern Virginia, 1861–1865*. An essay on the regiment, with an accompanying roster, was written by Robert J. Driver, Jr., and Kevin C. Ruffner in 1996 as part of the H.E. Howard Virginia Regimental series.

While the roles of the couriers may seem less glamorous than those of other troops, understanding their experiences and analyzing how they functioned are critical tools to understanding the larger war and to seeing how the Confederate army functioned in organization and structure. History often focuses on the grand charges and tragic last stands of war, yet the mundane, everyday aspects of army life and the functions of the many vital support and logistics elements have started to attract more interest over the last decade. This history of the Thirty-Ninth will, hopefully, continue to add to the ongoing effort to grasp exactly how Confederate military units worked. At the same time, it is an effort to document and preserve the unique experiences of a specific group of men whose service and sacrifice are no less worthy of history's attention because their duties were frequently commonplace ones. Like any other soldiers, they are worthy of study, and their story is worth telling.

As always, thanks go out to a variety of people: to National Park Service historians John Hennessy and Robert E.L. Krick, who answered numerous questions and provided documents. Special thanks to the librarians at William and Mary College, the Library of Virginia, the Virginia Historical Society, Handley Regional Library (Winchester), the Ruby B. Archie Public Library (Danville), Staunton Public Library and the Page Public Library. Charlie Knight, military curator at the North Carolina Museum of History, fielded many questions. A special thanks to Robert Moore for reading the manuscript, and, as always, to Elizabeth Baird Hardy. Words cannot express just how much you mean to me!

Chapter 1

1862

They were officially known as the Thirty-Ninth Battalion Virginia Cavalry, or as Major John H. Richardson's Battalion of Scouts, Guides and Couriers. Many considered themselves a part of Robert E. Lee's Body Guard. These varied names might imply that their notoriety rivaled that of Colonel John S. Mosby's Rangers, men who scouted in Northern Virginia, disrupting lines of communication and capturing supplies earmarked for Federal armies. Or perhaps they styled themselves as being similar to General Wade Hampton's Iron Scouts, who worked behind Union lines gathering intelligence and engaging in unconventional warfare. The Thirty-Ninth Battalion, while carrying names like Ewell's Body Guard and Lee's Body Guard, generally performed less exciting tasks. From available documentation, it seems these men seldom braved the cannon's fury in grand charges, although they were frequently under fire. They were, however, privileged witnesses to the war, interacting with the Army of Northern Virginia's high command on a daily basis.

Although they often receive little praise, couriers, guides and scouts were an essential part of the Confederate army. Confederate regulations laid out the duties of these men, referring to them as orderlies. At the beginning of a campaign, the army commander detailed a number of men, both mounted and on foot, to serve as couriers. They were ordered to convey messages to various commanders, although the regulations preferred that staff officers carry these messages unless the circumstance was "special and urgent." While staff officers carried orders, as prescribed in the regulations, the size of the armies, coupled with the number of messages being sent, forced army commanders to use the orderlies, or couriers, more frequently. The Thirty-Ninth carried messages for the generals to whom they were assigned. At the same time, they worked in telegraph offices, drove wagons and served as clerks in army headquarters.[3]

Early in the war, the Confederate high command would often detail companies from cavalry regiments to act in the roles of guides, scouts and couriers. According to J. Churchill Cooke, a sergeant in the Second Virginia Cavalry and member of the famed Hanover Troop (Dragoons), his company was pulled from the regiment and assigned to "different generals as guides, scouts, and couriers" during the Seven Days campaign. Unlike his messmates, Cooke was not originally from the lower part of Hanover County, Virginia. Due to his lack of familiarity with the topography, Cooke was assigned to bear Stonewall Jackson's headquarters flag. Cooke reported to Jackson, who told the sergeant "not to stay very close to him, only to keep him in sight." During the fight, Jackson called for Cooke with an order for J.E.B. Stuart. Cooke passed the flag to another orderly and set out to find the cavalry commander. Unsuccessful, he returned to the general and bore the flag for the remainder of the campaign.[4]

Federal activity in Virginia in the spring of 1862 brought an increase in Confederate forces. Robert E. Lee, working with Jefferson Davis, transferred regiments and brigades from other Southern states to combat the Federal military buildup. At the same time, the recently passed Conscription Act was forcing thousands to volunteer for Confederate service. New regiments were being created, and the Confederate army was swelling with new recruits.[5]

On May 1, 1862, William F. Randolph enlisted as a private in Company F, Sixth Virginia Cavalry. Born in 1831, Randolph was living with his mother and siblings on a farm in Fauquier County in 1860. Both of his grandfathers had served with distinction during the American Revolution. The Randolphs, relations of the Lee family, were quite wealthy, with almost $180,000 in personal property and real estate. William F. Randolph had spent several years in California mining gold before returning to Virginia in 1855. One year later, he was in Mississippi working a plantation using slaves given to him by his father, Robert. Randolph returned to Virginia at the commencement of hostilities. Based upon his surviving records, Private Randolph was detailed to serve nearly exclusively with Confederate general Richard S. Ewell from the starting date of his enlistment, serving as Ewell's courier during the battles of Port Republic and Cross Keys.[6]

The first company of Lee's Body Guard was organized for service under Major General Richard S. Ewell. *Library of Congress.*

Possibly at the urging of Ewell, Randolph received permission to raise a company of scouts and couriers in late July 1862. The company, later Company B of the Thirty-Ninth, was to be known as Ewell's Body Guard. Ewell wrote to Bradley T. Johnson, then commanding the First Maryland Infantry, asking the colonel to help Randolph fill his ranks. By mid-August, dozens of men had enlisted at Orange Court House to serve in Ewell's Body Guard. By August 18, there were forty-five men on the roster. Randolph was elected captain of the company. Thomas Turner, possibly a resident of Maryland, became first lieutenant. George Redmond, an Irish-born farmer living in Maryland in 1860, was elected second lieutenant. Charles E.A. Mount was also elected second lieutenant. Mount was thirty-four years old and a Loudoun County farmer. Redmond had already served nine months in the First Maryland Infantry. Mount had previously served as adjutant of the 132nd Virginia Militia. Turner apparently did not have any previous military service.[7]

Some of these new volunteers had previous Confederate military experience. John Cotter had enlisted in April 1861 in New Orleans in Wheat's Battalion, James B. Sinnot also served in a Louisiana regiment early in the war and Walter Rawlings claimed service with Sterling Price's men in Missouri. Several, like John Flannagan, Thomas Huffman and Joseph Heffley, were absent without leave from other commands when they enlisted in Ewell's Body Guard. The majority were farmers, and while there were a few foreign-born men in the ranks, most hailed from Virginia.[8]

While Randolph was working on organizing his company, Confederate forces in central Virginia were closely watching the Federal Army of Virginia under John Pope. Brought from a Federal command along the Mississippi River, Pope had adopted harsh measures toward Southern civilians in Virginia. He instructed his men to live off the land, while civilians were held responsible for damages caused by guerrilla attacks against his men. Lee sent the divisions of Jackson and Ewell, and, later, that of A.P. Hill, to deal with the "miscreant" Pope. Randolph's actions during the battle of Cedar Mountain are unknown, although there is no reason to believe that he and his men were not on the field.[9]

In late August, Jackson took his command toward the depot at Second Manassas. Elijah White, commander of the Thirty-Fifth Battalion Virginia Cavalry, gained permission from Ewell to lead a raid into Loudoun County on a search for Samuel C. Means's Loudoun Rangers, a Unionist company reportedly "harassing the people…severely." White's battalion was also known as "the Comanches." Supplementing the twenty Comanches were

Confederate general Thomas "Stonewall" Jackson and staff. Battles and Leaders.

Captain Randolph, Lieutenants Redmond and Mount, twenty members of Ewell's Body Guard and a handful of other scouts belonging to Jackson's command. The small band worked their way to the head of Jackson's advancing column and passed through the Bull Run Mountains at sunset on August 24. They spent the daylight hours of August 25 concealed, with local residents bringing them food. An hour before daylight on August 26, they reached Franklin's Mill, near the community of Waterford. Scouts were sent ahead, while White perfected his plan of attack. Means's men were using a local Baptist church as their base. Twenty of the Confederates were dismounted and placed under the command of Randolph. Their orders were to move toward the Baptist church and not fire until they were inside or at least within the churchyard. The remainder of White's force remained mounted.[10]

Dawn was just beginning to break as Randolph's men moved forward. Means's entire force was in the churchyard listening to a group of scouts reporting that there were no Confederates north of the Rappahannock River. As Randolph's men neared the churchyard, they opened fire, causing "the Yankees to break and rush into the house in great confusion." Randolph fell back a short distance, to the cover of a nearby house, while a handful of others rushed up to the windows and "poured their buckshot in." On hearing the firing, White's mounted troopers rode forward and fired a volley or two at the Federals leaping from other windows. White made a dash into town and captured a couple of Federals. Upon returning, White dismounted the rest of his men and demanded the surrender of the Federals in the church. They refused, and with ammunition starting to run short, White decided to kill the horses tethered nearby, preventing the Federals from following his small command. Before the mounts were dispatched, however, a white flag emerged from the church, and upon being assured that they would be released on parole, the Federals surrendered. Thirty were captured, along with "fifty-six horses, saddles and bridles, about one hundred fine revolvers and as many carbines, with a vast amount of plunder" that the Confederates were unable to carry. Losses were placed at "about seven or eight" Federals killed and wounded, while White's men lost two killed and several slightly wounded. No losses were reported for Randolph's company during the skirmish. However, Private Thomas Rock was reported wounded and was in an undisclosed hospital on September 1. The raiders were soon on their way back to Ewell and the rest of Jackson's command. The captured prisoners were sent to Richmond, while Ewell allowed White and Randolph to keep the captured horses for their own commands.[11]

There is no surviving account of the activities of Randolph's company during the battle of Second Manassas on August 28–30, 1862. Jackson's command had swung around Pope's army, capturing his supply depot at Manassas Junction. Jackson then fell back into a defensive position in the woods at Groveton near the old Manassas battlefield and dared the Federals to attack. Pope acquiesced and, believing Jackson to be both isolated and vulnerable, attacked. Jackson's line held. Longstreet arrived with his corps, deployed and, the next day, attacked Pope, driving his army back toward the defenses of Washington, D.C. During the battle, a minié ball shattered

General Ewell's right leg, a leg that Ewell subsequently lost. Soldiers bore Ewell behind the lines, and the next day, Frank Myers wrote that it was the Comanches who took the general to a house four miles from the battlefield. Campbell Brown, an officer on Ewell's staff, recorded in his memoir that after a week's stay near the battlefield, Ewell was moved to the home of his cousin near Haymarket, Virginia. The general was carried on a litter by "his faithful Hd. Qu. guard of 12 men who took it by turns of four at a time while one of us walked by his side & held an umbrella to shade his face." Many years after the war, Alice Ewell wrote that Ewell's Body Guard "were quartered at the entrance of our place, in the grove at 'Ewell's Chapel' on the Carolina Road," and that Captain Randolph took dinner with the family. Ewell would be absent for months. It is possible that other members of Randolph's company continued to serve Brigadier General Alexander R. Lawton, who took command of Ewell's division.[12]

In September 1862, William W. Page ran an advertisement in the *Richmond Daily Dispatch* stating he was recruiting a new company, later designated part of Company D, to be "Scouts, Guides and Couriers" for Robert E. Lee. The deadline for men coming in to enlist due to the conscription law had been extended, and Page was looking for men who had not yet signed up. Page encouraged the new recruits "to rally to the standard of your choice" instead of being forced into an unknown regiment. New recruits were promised the regular pay of a cavalry soldier, plus a fifty-dollar bounty. Page was born in 1840 in New York and was a student at Hampden-Sydney College when the war began. In May 1861, Page was mustered in as a first sergeant in the Twentieth Virginia Infantry and was captured at Rich Mountain that July. He was paroled two days later and was discharged from the regiment in March 1862. After the war, he claimed to have personally taken the matter of his parole to Robert E. Lee. He next appears as a first lieutenant of cavalry at Camp Lee in July 1862.[13]

At least twenty-six members of Page's command came from Camp Lee. Organized as a fairgrounds prior to the war and christened Camp Lee in honor of "Light Horse" Harry Lee in 1860, Camp Lee was a sixty-three-acre site dedicated to training Confederate soldiers. Jackson had marched the Virginia Military Institute cadets there in April 1861; William Gilham, who wrote an infantry manual, was the first camp commander; the grounds contained a hospital, quartermaster and commissary shops and rooms for surgeons and drill masters. It was also the site of executions for spies and deserters. Tens of thousands of volunteers and conscripts passed through the area during the four years of the war.[14]

GEN. R. E. LEE'S BODY GUARD.—FIFTY DOLLARS BOUNTY.—I am authorized to raise a company of cavalry for special service, as Scouts, Guides, and Couriers, with Gen. R. E. Lee. All persons not already in the service, or not actually enrolled as conscripts, will be received. A splendid chance for volunteering in a select corps is here offered.

The extension of the Conscript act will soon be enforced, and those between the ages of 35 and 45 called into service. You now have an opportunity of enlisting in a nice service. The honorable and advantageous nature of this service will recommend itself to all.

Everything furnished except horses. For further particulars, address me at Appomattox C. H.

J. W. LAWSON.

Lieuts. J. R. LAWSON, at Aspinwall, Charlotte, Va., and WM. H. MILNER, of Meadsville, Halifax, are authorized to receive members for this company.   [oc 4—6t*]   J. W. L.

From late 1862 through 1864, there were several announcements recruiting men for the Thirty-Ninth Battalion. Richmond Dispatch.

Headquarters at Camp Lee, a prewar camp utilized by Confederate forces for new recruits and conscripts. Harper's Weekly.

Page's activities for the next few months are shrouded in mystery. Listed as a private in a postwar roster of Mosby's Rangers, Page noted in June 1863 that his command, "in conjunction with Major Mosby," was engaged at Warren Junction. Losses were reported as one killed, three wounded and two captured. He was also engaged at Catlett's Station, presumably in May 1863, where Page himself was wounded in the right side of his neck. And then there were "sundry skirmishes in Loudoun, Fauquier, and [Culpeper] [Counties] without loss." Other activities that occurred between his newspaper advertisement in September 1862 and the beginning of summer 1863 seem to be lost to history.[15]

On September 24, 1862, John H. Richardson, former colonel of the Forty-Sixth Virginia Infantry, was tapped to command what was originally known as the Thirteenth Battalion Virginia Cavalry. That designation was later changed to the Thirty-Ninth Battalion Virginia Cavalry. Unofficially, it was Richardson's Battalion of Scouts, Guides and Couriers. Richardson was born in Richmond, Virginia, in 1828. He was a businessman, and before the war, he worked with streetcar companies in Cincinnati and St. Louis. He returned to Virginia by the early 1850s and organized a militia company known as the Young Guards. In 1856, his command was considered the "strongest" and "best drilled volunteer company in Virginia." By 1858, the Young Guards had grown to battalion strength, and Richardson was signing announcements as "Colonel, 179th Virginia Militia Regiment." Richardson's regiment honored Jefferson Davis with a salute when the president arrived in Richmond in May 1861. In June, Richardson volunteered for Confederate service, becoming a lieutenant colonel in the Second Regiment, Wise Legion. The regiment was later reorganized and designated the Forty-Sixth Virginia Infantry, with Richardson as lieutenant colonel. On May 20, 1862, Richardson was promoted to colonel of the regiment. For some unknown reason, Richardson was soon without a command. He penned a book on Confederate infantry tactics, and in September, he was assigned to Camp Lee and then designated as major of the Thirty-Ninth Battalion Virginia Cavalry.[16]

Other advertisements began to appear in Richmond newspapers. One in October 1862 promised a fifty-dollar bounty to new recruits for "Gen'l R. E. Lee's Body Guard." The new organization was considered "a select corps" and "a nice service." Everything they needed, save a horse, was provided to the new recruits. As per Confederate military requirements, mounts had to be purchased or brought from home. Men interested in joining before being conscripted could apply at Appomattox Court House, Aspinwall, Charlottesville or Richmond.[17]

A few members of Lee's Body Guard might have served with Colonel John S. Mosby. *Library of Congress.*

There were a handful of new recruits in September 1862, with most signing up to serve as members of Ewell's Body Guard. When October rolled around, twelve members of Randolph's company were reported absent without leave, with many never to return. On October 11, in Winchester, ninety-two men were mustered into Captain Pifer's Company of Scouts, Guides and Couriers (later Company A of the Thirty-Ninth). Commanding the company was Augustus P. Pifer, a native of Frederick County, Virginia, who was born in 1840. Pifer was a graduate of Roanoke College and was teaching prior to the war. He first served as adjutant of the Third Virginia Infantry, then in the Tenth Virginia Infantry, before being promoted and assigned to staff duty in Richmond. Pifer was elected captain the day the company was created. There appears to have been no first lieutenant in the company. Elected as second lieutenant was twenty-year-old William N. Green. He had already spent more than a year in service, first volunteering with the Forty-Ninth Virginia Infantry, then transferring to the Fauquier Artillery. George R. Balthrope rounded out the company-grade officers. He was born in Missouri and, prior to the war, was a forwarding agent on the Manassas Gap Railroad. As in Randolph's company, several of the men had previous military experience. A few were even absent without leave from other regiments when they enlisted in Pifer's company. Many of the men were from Frederick County, including three brothers, Joshua S., John R. and Thomas Lupton, along with their cousins John C. and J. Frank Lupton.[18]

It is possible that some of the men who were rolled into these new companies had seen prior service as couriers. Family accounts later claimed that Bean Campbell had served as a courier for months prior to the formation of Pifer's company. During the Romney campaign of January 1862, Campbell was sent by Jackson "around the mountain on a perilous ride through ice and snow" with orders "to tear up the railroad." When he delivered to Jackson the word that these orders had been carried out, Jackson responded with "Good; now go and get some sleep." Campbell had once delivered Lee's favorite mount, Traveler, and on another occasion, while serving at a signal post on Clark Mountain, had shared a "ham sandwich" that Lee had taken out of the "back pocket of his coat."[19]

A later historian wrote that "every section of the border was represented, and the battalion could furnish competent guides and couriers on all occasions." Many of the men in Captain Randolph's company were reportedly from Fairfax, Prince William, Albemarle and other counties in northern Virginia, while those in Captain Pifer's company hailed from the lower Shenandoah Valley counties of Frederick and Clarke. Page's men came from Pittsylvania, Buckingham and neighboring counties. If Lee or another general needed a scout or courier, having so many men from different communities would be beneficial, as they might be familiar with the topography.[20]

Toward the end of 1862, others were attempting to recruit companies to serve as guides, couriers and scouts for the Army of Northern Virginia. John W. Jackson called upon former Hampden-Sydney students to join a cavalry company, later part of Company D, for "special service." Jackson was then in Fluvanna County. In Richmond, recruiters were looking for "young, ambitious, and enterprising spirits, and dashing riders." New recruits were promised a "horse, perfect outfit, and $50 bounty." To those who enlisted, "Ample opportunity to win laurels in the most attractive service in the army" was promised. All that was required was to report to the recruiting office opposite Spotswood Hotel.[21]

Robert E. Lee was anxious to have his battalion of scouts, guides and couriers in the field. From Fredericksburg, he wrote to Major Richardson on November 30 to ask how the organization was going and telling Richardson that Captain Pifer's company had arrived the day before. The next day, he wrote to Secretary of War James A. Seddon about the decline in effective cavalry troops. The war was taking its toll on horses, and exorbitant prices were keeping the veteran cavalrymen from procuring new mounts. Lee then provided the strongest evidence for the creation of the Thirty-Ninth Battalion Virginia Cavalry: "At present many of the cavalry are detached from their regiments as couriers for general and staff officers of the army. Couriers are necessary for an army serving in the field, and I had hoped to supply the places of the cavalry by a corps of guides and couriers authorized to be raised by the President…to the command which Colonel Richardson, of Virginia, has been assigned." He wanted a new regulation to prevent regular cavalry from serving as couriers, while at the same time, he believed that generals should "mount a few men of their own commands to act as couriers." Seddon wrote back, stating that President Jefferson Davis agreed with Lee; using cavalry "as couriers for general and staff officers" was "injudicious, and should be stopped." Lee could issue the order, or the regulation could be modified.[22]

Obviously, Captain Randolph's company arrived soon after Pifer's company. When Jubal Early penned his official report for the battle of Fredericksburg, he praised many of his staff officers, including Randolph. Early commanded Ewell's Division. During the battle, Early wrote, Randolph accompanied him on the field and displayed "coolness, courage,

Lee observing the battle of Fredericksburg. *Library of Congress.*

and intelligence," lending Early aid and bearing his orders to his brigade commanders. However, the precise role Randolph and the other members of his company played during the battle is unknown. At Fredericksburg, Confederate forces were dug in on hills above the town. On December 13, Federal forces, now under the command of Ambrose Burnside, launched several attacks on various portions of the Confederate defenses. On the Confederate right, the Federals were able to break part of the Confederate line, but reinforcements quickly pushed the Federals back across the field, resulting in a costly Federal defeat.[23]

Captain Pifer reported that his company was deployed in the rear during the battle, charged with arresting and returning stragglers to their commands. Three days after the battle, Pifer's command started for Richmond, "having in charge between four and five hundred prisoners." They marched their prisoners to Hanover Junction, where they boarded a train to Richmond. Pifer's men were back with the army by December 18, having covered a distance of 140 miles.[24]

A few days after the battle, Early submitted a field return for men present in Ewell's division. Randolph's company reported three officers and fifty-eight enlisted men present for duty, with thirteen men absent. The number present with Captain Pifer is unknown. As 1862 ended, Lee had two companies of his "corps of guides and couriers" in the field, with others on the way. Major Richardson was in command. Ewell's Body Guard, commanded by William Randolph, became Company B. Augustus Pifer's command became Company A. The Thirty-Ninth Battalion Virginia Cavalry was taking shape.[25]

Chapter 2

1863

L ife settled into a somewhat dull routine following the battle of Fredericksburg. The Confederate army went into winter quarters along the Rappahannock River, watching the Army of the Potomac on the other side. "We have very little to do and plenty to eat," reported Sergeant John Lupton (Company A). Couriers rotated on and off various assignments. Captain Pifer reported that two men were detailed for the army telegraph office and the medical board. Some of the assignments were of a more permanent duration. Soon after enlisting in Company A, Joshua Lupton was detailed as a wagon master to Robert E. Lee's personal wagon train, a position he held until at least the end of 1864. Likewise, Anthony Butts (Company B) was detailed to drive Lee's ambulance in August 1863. Many saw the role of a teamster as light duty. John Lupton wrote to those back home about his brother's assignment: Joshua "has the easiest place in the Army having nothing to do but issue forage to General Lee's horses twice a day."[26]

Colonel Walter Taylor, one of Lee's staff officers, described the headquarters of the Army of Northern Virginia as consisting of "five or six army-tents, one or two wagons for transporting equipage and personal effects, with no display of bunting, and no parade of sentinels or guards, only a few orderlies." Francis Dawson, a member of Lieutenant General James Longstreet's staff, wrote that there "was no pomp or circumstance about [Lee's] headquarters, and no sign of rank of the occupant, other than the Confederate flag displayed in front of the tent of Colonel Taylor." Quite possibly the best description of Lee's headquarters comes from a British officer sent to observe the war. While still in Winchester, before the battle of Fredericksburg, this observer found Lee and his staff quartered "in seven or eight pole tents....In front of the tents were some three or four wheeled wagons, drawn up without any regularity, and a number of horses roamed loose about the field...the mounted soldiers called 'couriers,' who always accompany each general of division in the field, were unprovided with tents, and slept in or under the wagons." Compared to those of generals from past conflicts (or even to those of other Confederate commanders), Lee's headquarters were simple.[27]

It appears that Company A was working for General Lee in early 1863. John Lupton wrote in February 1863 that Lee had ordered all of the old couriers back to their respective commands. Lupton's compatriots were rotating on and off of duty with the commanding general. "We furnish from ten to twenty men each day," he wrote. "I go to Headquarters tomorrow morning with a squad of men and return the next day to camp." His brother Thomas believed they were "doing some pretty hard dewty [sic]." A few days before, they had escorted conscripts to General Jackson's command. Captain Pifer reported at the end of February that his company, besides delivering messages or driving wagons, was scouring the countryside. In two months, they had collected "38,000 rounds of ammunition for small arms; several hundred stands of arms, bayonets, etc. These quartermaster stores and ordnance stores were left scattered through the country partly by our own army and partly by the enemy last summer."[28]

On March 9, 1863, Captain Randolph's company was officially assigned to Richardson's Battalion of Scouts, Guides and Couriers, although it was on duty before that date. It would officially become known as Company B, Thirty-Ninth Battalion Virginia Cavalry. By this point in time, the company was being referred to as General Jackson's Escort. Exactly when it moved from Ewell's division to corps headquarters is not clear. Work continued on recruiting additional companies. Albert H. Pettigrew and Samuel B. Brown were both recruiting for a company for "Lee's Body Guard." Ten men joined the new company in November, fourteen in December, twenty-three in January, sixteen in February and ten more in March. On March 9, the company was formally organized, with Brown elected captain. Born in 1842 in Augusta County, Brown attended the University of Virginia prior to the war. He enlisted in the Fifty-Second Virginia Infantry in July 1861 and worked his way up from a junior second lieutenant to captain, commanding Company K. Brown was wounded in the foot at the battle

Robert E. Lee (*center*), Walter Taylor (*right*) and G.W.C. Lee (*left*) in an image taken a few days after the surrender at Appomattox. *Library of Congress.*

of Port Republic and subsequently forced to resign in February 1863. A month later, he was well enough to take command of a company of scouts and couriers. Albert Pettigrew was elected first lieutenant. Born in 1841 in Botetourt County, Pettigrew was listed as a student in the 1860 census. John

H. Lionberger, a Virginia Military Institute student born in Luray in 1843, was elected second lieutenant. Lionberger had already seen service in the Seventh Virginia Cavalry and the Dixie Artillery before joining the Thirty-Ninth Battalion Virginia Cavalry. Filling the role of third lieutenant was Andrew J. Broaddus. A possible Kentucky native, Broaddus appears not to have had previous military experience.[29]

One of those new recruits for Brown's company was Isaac Hite. It took Hite seven days to travel from his home in Page County to Camp Lee. Traveling in February, he complained of the snow, "about ten inches here." There were tents for the soldiers, but the horses had no shelter. Rations for horses were "a gallon and a half of corn, and about 12 lbs of hay per day." However, Hite and his messmates received "very slim" rations, "a small piece of bread, a little sugar and rice, and a very small piece of bacon" every day. Often, soldiers formed themselves into small groups, or messes, to handle camp chores like cooking. Hite was writing on February 23. Elections for officers had just been held. "There were a great many office seekers here which created some little disturbance before the election," he told his father. While there were fifty-eight men present, they needed seventy-three men to be officially mustered. Lionberger headed back to Page County, and Brown was sent to Staunton, each to recruit more men. Hite wrote again on March 21—his company had just been mustered into service, but the men had not yet received their equipment. It was wet, cold and windy, and the horses were still without shelter. "We get plenty of grain for them though hardly enough long feed." Hite thought his own rations were "yet very short. We sometimes eat all that we draw for all day, and then [fast] the balance of the day or buy something."[30]

For the next couple of months, life was a dull routine: rotating on and off duty, taking care of their horses and seeking better food. The Lupton brothers wrote of buying shad to supplement their army fare: "We had for supper last night light biscuit plus shad and coffee. For breakfast this morning, light biscuit and shad and coffee. For supper this evening, biscuit-fried ham and sweet potatoes. But we do not live in this way all the time. But we have plenty of bread and meat all ways." Many soldiers used their free time to write letters home, while others worked on their next meal. For all of the men in the army, their thoughts were turning toward the spring campaign.[31]

The Confederate army in Virginia had faced several different Union commanders. General Irvin McDowell led the failure at First Manassas. He was replaced by General George B. McClellan, whose grand scheme to take Richmond from the east failed in a series of battles known as the

Seven Days in June and July 1862. General John Pope commanded a force whipped by Lee, Jackson and Longstreet in August 1862. McClellan was again tapped to command the Federal army in September and was able to fight Lee to a draw along the banks of Antietam Creek. General Ambrose Burnside replaced McClellan, but his defeat at Fredericksburg led to ghastly Federal losses. General Joseph Hooker replaced Burnside as commander of the Army of the Potomac in early 1863. Hooker reportedly told a newspaper editor: "The rebel army is now the legitimate property of the Army of the Potomac. They may as well pack up their haversacks and make for Richmond. I shall be after them."[32]

Leaving a force the size of Lee's army at Fredericksburg, Hooker crossed over the Rappahannock and Rapidan Rivers forty miles upstream. By the evening of April 30, close to eighty thousand Federal soldiers were in Lee's rear. Instead of retreating toward Richmond, Lee left a small force in the Fredericksburg defenses and moved toward the Chancellorsville village. After a series of sharp, small counterattacks, Hooker lost his nerve and fell back toward Chancellorsville, ordering his men to entrench. With most of Longstreet's command absent, Lee and Jackson had to devise a plan. While Lee remained behind with a few troops to keep Hooker's attention, Jackson was poised to move his entire corps on a circuitous route that pitched his troops against Hooker's weak right flank. At one point on April 30, Lee came to Captain Pifer and ordered him to send thirty men toward a ford over an unnamed stream or river. Federal cavalry had crossed over, and according to Thomas Lupton, Pifer's men had "a pretty hard time of it as they were skirmishing all day." During the fight, Pifer "had a ball to cut his cape and one of the boys had his horse killed." When forced to "skidaddle" by Federal cavalry, "our Lieutenant's horse fell down and hurt him rite badly."[33]

Captain Randolph's company was attached to Jackson's command during the campaign. Randolph was personally with Jackson for much of the day on May 2. According to Randolph, Jackson ordered him ahead to scout the Federal position. Taking one other trooper with him, he rode toward the Federal flank, keenly looking for their pickets. When Randolph spied the fire of the Federal camps, he dismounted and quietly moved ahead to the edge of a field. There, Randolph "saw a sight most amazing….No less than a vast force of Federals in every conceivable state of disorder, without any formation; several batteries of artillery unlimbered; hundreds gathered around the camp fires cooking, some sunning themselves in the bright May sunshine…no sentinels, no pickets, no line of battle anywhere." Randolph retrieved his horse and quickly rode to Jackson with the intelligence.[34]

Robert E. Lee approved Jackson's attack at Chancellorsville, then led part of the covering attack. *Library of Congress.*

Private Lloyd Smith was reportedly a part of Jackson's party when the general was wounded. *Michael C. Hardy.*

Jackson deployed two divisions and launched his attack, rolling up the flank of the Federal army. As darkness settled in the thick woods, Jackson's attack sputtered to a halt. He called for his reserve—A.P. Hill's Light Division—still stacked in a column on the Orange Plank Road. General James H. Lane's Tar Heel brigade was in the lead and deployed forward. One regiment fanned out as skirmishers while two regiments went into the line of battle to the right of the road and two to the left of the road. Lane then rode back to look for Hill and further orders. Instead of Hill, Lane found Jackson, who ordered him to push ahead into the darkness. Lane then headed to the right of his line to get the attack moving. Unbeknownst to Lane, Jackson and his staff rode ahead into the darkness, possibly as far as the skirmish line, listening to the enemy soldiers who were constructing breastworks. Along with Randolph, Jackson's party that evening included two additional members of the Thirty-Ninth Battalion: Privates Joshua Johns and Lloyd Smith, plus five others.[35]

Confusion reigned supreme in the tangled woods along the Orange Plank Road. On Lane's right, the 128th Pennsylvania Infantry stumbled into Confederate lines. In the darkness, four Tar Heels captured almost two hundred members of the Pennsylvania regiment. Out front, along the skirmish line, a Federal officer rode close by, calling out for his general.

Confederate skirmishers opened fire, which the Federals returned. Hearing further commotion to their right, Lane's men opened fire. Muskets and rifles blazed out into the darkness. "Order those men to stop that fire, and tell the officers not to allow another shot fired without orders," Randolph recalled Jackson saying. Randolph stated that he rode behind the ranks of Tar Heels, ordering them not to fire. He found his task in vain: "Those immediately in front would cease as I gave the order, but the firing would break out above or below me, and instead of ceasing, the shots increased in frequency." Randolph rode back to Jackson, encouraging the general to return behind Confederate lines. As Jackson turned his horse toward Confederate lines, another member of his party, possibly Lieutenant Joseph G. Morrison, his aide-de-camp and brother-in-law, likewise rode toward the Confederate lines: "Cease firing! You are firing into our own men," called out the officer. "Who gave that order?" questioned a major in one of Lane's regiments. "It's a lie! Pour it into them, boys!" And with that, the Tar Heels again lit up the woods with a more concentrated volley.[36]

Writing after the war, Randolph recalled seeing a "long line of bayonets rise and concentrate upon us." Sensing what was happening, he dug his spurs into the flanks of his horse, jumping the animal high in the air. "I looked back as my horse made the leap, and everything had gone down like leaves before the blast of a hurricane.…My own horse was wounded in several places, my clothing and saddle were perforated with bullets, yet I escaped without a wound." After regaining control of his horse, Randolph rushed back, spotting Jackson's horse on the side of the road. Randolph dismounted and found Jackson lying in the woods. He raised the stricken general, asking him if he was hurt, and Jackson replied, groaning, "Wild fire, that sir; wild fire." Randolph stated that Jackson was shot in the left arm and right hand. A.P. Hill, who was also out in front of the lines but survived the volley, soon arrived and ordered Randolph to go find an ambulance. Besides Jackson, Joshua Johns of the Thirty-Ninth Battalion was wounded. His horse bolted toward Federal lines, and he was captured.[37]

According to Randolph, he mounted and rushed toward the rear. "I soon found two of the ambulance corps with a stretcher, and ordered them to the front, saying a wounded officer needed their services. Then I rode further on to find an ambulance." Randolph ran into another member of Jackson's staff, who sent him to find J.E.B. Stuart. Randolph later wrote that

Captain William F. Randolph was supposedly with Jackson on the night he was wounded. Battles and Leaders.

I rode off through the woods in the direction of the river [Rappahannock], *and by a piece of good luck soon struck a well defined road, which seemed to lead in the right direction. After riding along that road for a few miles, I had the good fortune to meet General Stuart himself, with a small escort of cavalry. I stated that General Jackson had been badly wounded, and that Pendleton had ordered me to tell him to come to the army at once. Without making any comment he dashed off at full speed. I tried to follow, but by this time my horse was much weakened by the loss of blood and began to stagger under me. I was obliged to dismount and found that he was shot through both thighs and slightly wounded in several places, so I was forced to walk, leading the wounded animal slowly behind me.*[38]

Stuart would go on to lead Jackson's corps in the bloody attacks on May 3. Eventually, Hooker's line at Chancellorsville broke, and the Federals withdrew a mile back toward the Rappahannock River. Hooker crossed the river again on the night of May 5 and the early morning of May 6, and the Chancellorsville campaign ended. Many consider Chancellorsville Lee's greatest victory. But it came at a staggering loss. Among the ten thousand casualties was Jackson, who died on May 10.

The actions of other members of the Thirty-Ninth Battalion are largely unknown. George Smith (Company B) was reportedly wounded in the head and sent to a hospital in Richmond. Lloyd Smith's horse was killed at the same time Jackson was wounded. He believed the round that struck his horse also struck Stonewall. Philip Smith's horse was killed on May 3. John Hall's postwar obituary stated he was on his way to Jackson with a message when the general was struck. Thomas Williamson, apparently a member of the yet-to-be-formed Company D, was wounded and captured. According to Isaac Hite, Captain Brown's company reported for duty on April 30. They were ordered to guard prisoners, round up stragglers and guard the surrounding roads. On the night of May 3, they were ordered to escort 650 Federal prisoners to Guinea Station, along with an additional 200 more on May 4. Hite and his company probably boarded a train at Guinea Station and escorted the prisoners to Richmond.[39]

Over the next six weeks, the three companies in the battalion continued to work on their organization. Captain Pifer's company was at Culpeper with eighty-three horses. On May 22, Brown's company was reported to be in Fredericksburg with seventy-five horses available for duty. On June 15, he requested a wall tent, wagon, horses, harnesses, wagon saddle and other items. Thomas Marks was appointed as the battalion's assistant surgeon

Stonewall Jackson's final resting place is in Lynchburg, Virginia. *Michael C. Hardy.*

on June 3. Born in Alabama in 1838, Marks attended both Cumberland University and Tulane University before moving to Texas in 1860, where he practiced medicine. Marks was originally mustered in as a private in the Ninth Louisiana Infantry in March 1862 and was captured in the fighting at Fredericksburg on May 3, 1863. Soon after his parole, he was assigned to the Thirty-Ninth Battalion.[40]

Following the death of Jackson, Lee chose to reorganize his army. James Longstreet continued to command the First Corps; Richard Ewell was promoted and assigned to command the Second Corps; and Ambrose Powell Hill assumed command of the newly created Third Corps. Ideally, there should have been a company of the Thirty-Ninth Battalion assigned to each of the three corps, plus one to Lee himself. Only three companies were actually in the field. In postwar years, several men claimed to have served with

Lee, Jackson and Ewell. Only one, Joseph Chumby, claimed to have served with Longstreet. During the war, there were several who were reported to be with Major General George Pickett of Longstreet's corps. Undoubtedly, troopers were assigned to other commands, but that information appears to have been lost over the years.[41]

In early June, Lee chose to move the Army of Northern Virginia north into Pennsylvania. He wanted to draw the Federal army after him, permitting Virginia farmers to cultivate their crops and allowing his men to live off an area untouched by the hand of war. Furthermore, he was hoping a victory or two on Northern soil would alleviate the pressure being applied to Confederate forces along the Mississippi River. Plus, a victory in the North might force the Lincoln administration to negotiate an end to the war or lead to European recognition and alliances.

Lee's army set out on June 3. Hill's corps was left behind in Fredericksburg to watch the Federal army. Soon, Joseph Hooker, who commanded at Chancellorsville, was replaced by General George G. Meade. Isaac Hite (Company C) reported arriving in Culpeper Court House on June 7. He had "no time to write at present." While Lee believed cavalry companies should be with their commands, he was not above pulling men out for special duty. John Gill, a Marylander who was serving in the First Battalion Maryland Cavalry, was detailed with several others to serve as scouts and couriers prior to the Gettysburg Campaign. They were attached to Ewell's command. "To be assigned to duty at the headquarters of a general commanding a corps was quite an elevation for us," Gill wrote after the war. "We anticipated pleasant military experiences, which were more than realized before we got through the Gettysburg campaign." Gill's comrades served as provosts and rearguards before being ordered back to their command in mid-July.[42]

Over the course of the next three weeks, Lee's troops worked their way from Virginia across Maryland and into Pennsylvania. One private, Franklin Walter (Company A), kept a diary recording the movements of Captain Pifer's command. Walter recorded that on June 22, he attended Berryville Episcopal Church with Lee and Longstreet. On June 25, Lee crossed the Potomac at the head of his company of the Thirty-Ninth Battalion and camped near Williamsport. The following day, they were seven miles north of Hagerstown, Maryland. Walter rotated duty with those couriers assigned to Lee on June 27, following Lee through Greencastle and Chambersburg. The general issued two orders concerning the campaign. The first set forth proper foraging procedures. Goods were to be bought at fair market value, and the property of private citizens had to be respected. In the second order,

Lee reminded his men that they were not waging war upon unarmed and defenseless people. Any soldier caught abusing private property would be arrested and punished. John Rodes (Company C) recalled after the war that Lee's orders were "rigidly enforced," and punishment followed whenever culprits were caught. On "one occasion while passing through Pennsylvania Gen. Lee came upon several of his soldiers," Rodes recalled, "who were in cherry trees, satisfying their hunger." Lee stopped, and then sent a courier "to the owner of the cherries to ask permission before he would touch one of them. The lady of the house not only consented but on hearing that Gen. Lee had made the request, sent a waiter [sic] of strawberries to the Confederate chieftain, and went in person to extend the permission asked."[43]

Franklin Walter found his company camped one mile east of Chambersburg on the evening of June 28. Lee learned that day that the Federal army was north of the Potomac River and ordered his own scattered corps to move toward Cashtown and Gettysburg. Private Walter wrote of camping eight miles east of Chambersburg on the Baltimore Road on June 29. The armies continued their trek toward Gettysburg on June 30, with minor skirmishes between the Confederates and local militias. In one of those skirmishes, Federal troopers belonging to the Sixteenth Pennsylvania Cavalry swooped into Greencastle in the rear of the Confederate lines. They found Confederate mail, payroll records and $8,000 in cash, as well as several Confederates. Among the captured were Privates John Hall (Company A) and Charles Caldwell (Company C). Hall, "while on a special mission…was captured and imprisoned." It is possible that one of these prisoners was mentioned in a report by General John Buford. Writing to Major General John F. Reynolds, Buford told of capturing "a courier of Lee's. Nothing was found on him." However, Buford managed to discover from the prisoner that Ewell's corps was moving through Carlisle with Robert Rodes's division nearby.[44]

Confederate and Union forces clashed at Gettysburg on July 1. "[W]e could hear the rapid firing of artillery and musketry in the direction of Gettysburg," Walter recorded in his diary. After severe fighting west and north of Gettysburg, Federal forces were pushed out of town and into a defensive position on a ridge south of town. Later that afternoon, Lee's wagons stopped on the Chambersburg Pike and unloaded the headquarters tents and baggage. Sergeant Martin Gander (Company C) recalled that he "placed four guards around the old stone house on the hill, the personal headquarters of Gen. Lee the evening of July 1, 1863 about 5:30 pm. at the command of Adjutant General Taylor, who was in the field headquarters

Tradition states that Lee used this building for a meeting during the battle of Gettysburg. *Library of Congress.*

across the street." This structure was known as the Thompson House. Colonel Charles Marshall, of Lee's staff, remembers that "General Lee slept that night [July 1] in a small stone house east of Seminary Ridge and just north of the Chambersburg Pike, his staff bivouacking in an orchard near by."[45]

Couriers undoubtedly flew back and forth across the fields around Gettysburg, bearing messages to various commanders. Generals occasionally made mention of couriers but seldom recorded their names. The exact roles of many of these of these men remain lost pieces of history. James Denny (Company A) wrote after the war that he was detailed to deliver a note to Longstreet ordering him to push his attack. Denny wrote that he moved some three miles between lines of infantry and cavalry to reach Longstreet.

This monument, erected around 1920 or 1921 on the Gettysburg battlefield, marks the spot of Lee's official headquarters. *Michael C. Hardy.*

Then, Denny returned to headquarters: "His horse was panting when he got back to Lee's Headquarters and he admitted that he was trembling, too, for shells were bursting around him and the roar of musketry was deafening." Lieutenant William Green (Company A) and Captain Samuel Brown both reported that parts of their companies were assigned to the engineers who were out learning the roads and engaged in reconnaissance. It is entirely possible that many of the Thirty-Ninth Battalion never saw the field. Franklin Walter (Company A) reported being camped one and a half miles from Gettysburg on the evening of July 1. On July 2, he was ordered two miles to the rear, then one and a half miles toward the front, where he "remained… on picket duty until after dark." The private could hear the "skirmishing in [the] front which began early in the morning [and] continued brisk until 4 o'clock when the firing became terrific. Artillery and musketry engaged along the whole line." At nine that evening, he returned to camp. While he could hear the battle, he spent July 3 again staffing a picket post. In addition to the two privates who were captured early in the action, losses for the Thirty-Ninth Battalion at Gettysburg were one killed, two wounded and nine captured. One of the wounded was Major Richardson, who suffered a "severe saber cut" at some point during the battle.[46]

The plaque on Lee's headquarters' marker at Gettysburg. *Michael C. Hardy.*

On July 4, Lee began pulling out his army and heading back to Virginia. Private Walter recalled being awakened by a sergeant at 3:00 a.m, and sent to Doctors Guild and McGuire with messages undoubtedly related to the withdrawal of the Confederate army. When Walter returned, he found many of his company now "armed with long range guns," presumably Springfield and Enfield rifles. Walter was soon detailed to serve in the escort for Lee's headquarters wagons and started off at 2:00 p.m. in "a drenching rain." They stopped around 6:00 p.m. near the Black Horse Inn and set off again about midnight. At daylight, they were at Fairfield. Walter recorded that they "suffered intensely awhile before day for want of sleep often nodding on my horse and several times coming near falling." Upon finding a tannery nearby, Walter went to sleep on a plank, probably to keep out of the mud. After a few hours of sleep for the men and rest for the horses, the headquarters wagons moved on. By the morning of July 7, the caravan was within two miles of Hagerstown, Maryland.[47]

Campbell Brown, on the staff of General Ewell, recalled that a couple of days out from Gettysburg, rations were exhausted. Another staff member, Elliott Johnson, was sent out with "a small escort from his Courier Company, & some wagons, to forage." They came across one farm and demanded

Lieutenant General James Longstreet played a critical role in the battle of Gettysburg. *Library of Congress.*

the keys to the smokehouse. The "old woman" at home refused and placed herself in front of the building. Johnson "had her moved & the door smashed--took bacon &c., even to 50 or 60 lbs. sausage…got flour…[and] as the result of his days trip brought back about one day's rations for the Corps."[48]

Franklin Walter was assigned to Lee's party on July 7 and found the general two miles beyond Hagerstown. The party moved on side roads and through fields. At 2:00 p.m., Private Walter was sent to Longstreet's camp, riding nearly to Williamsport before returning, apparently unable to find the general. That evening, he went to sleep in the "open air and was awakened by rain falling on me." He moved to a tent fly, where he "slept soundly." The next day, Walter found it raining very hard. The water was "dripping through the tent and running under me." Mounting his horse, he rode two miles before he found something to eat, then returned to camp. Lee's army was bedraggled by the rain. It had swollen the Potomac River, and Lee was unable to cross with his army. Federal cavalry had destroyed a pontoon bridge over the Potomac days earlier. The Army of Northern Virginia was trapped at Williamsport as they waited for a new bridge to be built and for the waters to recede.[49]

From Hagerstown, John Lupton (Company A) wrote home on July 9 about the recent campaign. "We have had some very hard times since we left home," he wrote to his parents. At Gettysburg, the Confederate army had "ran a fowl [sic] of the enemy where a fight took place which lasted three days." The battle of Gettysburg was the "hardest fight of the war," and the Federals "had the finest position…you ever saw and we the poorest." After killing and wounding thousands, the "fighting just stopped each army holding its position." In Lupton's opinion, General Stuart had "made one of the finest raids the world ever saw. He captured two hundred and thirty-horse, six hundred mules and about three thousand wagons." Lupton ended his letter with: "I do not believe there is a boy in the company [who] would have missed this trip for $1,000." Isaac Hite (Company C) had a different take on the battle. His brother John, serving in a different regiment, was killed in the fighting. "Gen Lee was evidently driven out of Maryland," Isaac wrote in mid-July, "and on the whole I consider the trip a total failure, for he certainly expected to go further than he did, and not come back as soon as he did. The few cattle and horses that were captured will not begin to pay for our losses, besides the army at this time is in very low sp[i]rits."[50]

On July 10, portions of the Thirty-Ninth Battalion were able to cross the river. The next day, detachments from Pifer's and Brown's companies moved beyond Georgetown, spreading out in "four squads on different roads looking for stragglers." Richardson's battalion was obviously strung out over a large area. General Lee wrote to General Stuart that same day, reporting that "Captain Randolph, commanding courier company, of General Ewell's corps, who is on the Greencastle road, and 3 miles from the Pennsylvania line, reports: 'No enemy, and no report of any.'" Captain Brown reported that his command escorted prisoners from Winchester to Staunton and, later, with twenty men, gathered two hundred stragglers in the Bunker Hill area. Lee's army finished crossing the Potomac River on July 14, and the Gettysburg campaign came to an end for the Thirty-Ninth as well as for the rest of the Confederate army.[51]

Lee had little time to rebuild and refit his command. Federal forces crossed the Potomac River at Harpers Ferry on July 17, 1863, advancing up the Loudoun Valley. They eventually arrived at Manassas Gap, protecting the Federal capital and putting pressure on Lee's supply lines. Lee moved two corps through Front Royal and toward the vicinity of Culpeper. Franklin Walter recorded on July 16 that he was at headquarters with nothing to do. After a day off, he reported to Longstreet's headquarters. On July 20, Longstreet sent Walter to Lee with a message. It took Walter four hours to find Lee and deliver the message. The next morning, Lee sent Walter back to Longstreet with a reply. Walter "arrived at Winchester at 10 A.M My horse very tired." After resting and feeding his horse, Walter set out an hour later: "Went 5 miles on Millwood road. Heard that Gen. Longstreet had gone to Front Royal. Turned back and went to F. R. road. Arrived at Front Royal sundown very broken down. Gave dispatch to another courier." Walter went to a local house to rest, and, while there, "my saddle pockets containing my clothing, overcoat and gum blanket were stolen from my saddle." He was back in the saddle at 10:00 p.m., noting that the other courier also failed to find Longstreet. Finally, Walter located Longstreet the next morning: "4-1/2 miles from Front Royal on Chester Gap road." Walter stayed with Longstreet as the latter moved to Culpeper Court House. The courier was rotated off duty on July 25.[52]

At the end of August, Major Richardson reported five companies present, including Pifer's Company A, Randolph's Company B and Pettigrew's Company C. Also probably present were the two detachments under William Page and John Jackson. The consolidation of those two companies would not take place until the middle of 1864. Lieutenant Page was reported to be wounded in a skirmish near Catlett's Station late in the summer of 1863.[53]

Active campaigning started again on September 1. On September 8, two divisions of Longstreet's corps were transferred to Tennessee to bolster the command of General Braxton Bragg and the Army of Tennessee. Federal cavalry and infantry crossed the Rappahannock River on September 13, establishing their headquarters at Culpeper Court House. Bragg's victory at Chickamauga and the subsequent Federal decision to ship two corps west convinced Lee that it was time to do something. In October, he attempted to flank the Federal position. One of Ewell's staff officers recalled a new courier: "Christman" (possibly Nathaniel Christian) led Johnson's division "too far towards Culpeper" on October 12, costing the Confederates some time. Fighting erupted near Bristoe Station on October 14, chewing up two Confederate brigades and costing the Confederates a battery of artillery. Thomas Lupton (Company A) recalled in a letter home that he was "on duty at Headquarters and was riding all day and that morning[;] we were exposed to some shelling, but came through safe." Ewell's corps captured "about 170" Federals after the battle. Lieutenant Oliver Price (Company B) "with 8 or 9 of our Courier Co. got 74." John Lupton recalled from a camp near Culpeper Court House following the campaign that "the army has been marching for some time." His company had been on prisoner detail. "We came here last night after three days march with some prisoners we brought upwards of 600. We marched them very hard. We left three or four of them dead on the road." Lee was unable to make any headway against the Federal army and chose to fall back, tearing up the Orange and Alexandria Railroad.[54]

A couple of weeks of rest followed, and many hoped the armies would stop active campaigning and settle into winter quarters. Thomas Lupton wrote home on November 1:

> *We are camped about eight miles northeast of Culpeper Court House and about one and a half miles from Brandy Station on the Orange and Alexander [sic] railroad. Since we have been hear [sic], we have had a prety [sic] good time as we'nt much to do and plenty of rations and pretty good pasture for our horses....We have been for last two days employed in building us a house of logs which we will have got done all but daubing the cracks and when we are done we will have splendid quarters for the winter if we can only stay atar. I think we will stay for some time yet as they are putting up chimneys to their tents at headquarters....I like to have fogotten to tell you that we have splendid brick chimney to our house.*[55]

Late in November, the Federal army attempted to steal a march on Lee and strike the right flank of the Confederate army south of the Rapidan River. At the end of the first day's fighting, Confederates held their positions. That night, Lee's men moved back to a better position along Mine Run. The Federals attacked but found Confederate defenses too strong and withdrew during the night of December 1–2.

The men of Richardson's battalion were wrapped up in their roles as scouts, guides and couriers. At times, they were sent out to look for stragglers. At other times, they sought lost horses. Sergeant Samuel Wood (Company D) ran an advertisement in a Richmond newspaper describing his lost horse and offering a fifty-dollar reward. John Lupton wrote that Captain Pifer's horses came up missing one morning. Three men from Company A were detailed to look for missing animals. "We rode until nearly dark when we put up at an old man's by the name of Morton who has a son in our company." After Morton refused to be paid the next morning for keeping the soldiers, the three rode on, and it is unclear if they ever caught the missing horses. When Longstreet headed west, his couriers were sent back to their respective companies. One member of the battalion was at the telegraph office when a message arrived about the battle of Chickamauga. The courier sped down the road to find Lee, who, upon receiving the missive, sat on his horse in the road to examine it while "the couriers stopped a piece behind him while he read it. When he got through, he turned and said to the boys 'come up, good news, Brag[g] had gained a compleat [sic] victory over the enemy.'"[56]

There was much monotony in the lives of the men of the Thirty-Ninth. "John and Johnny are a short distance of[f] trying to catch lice, but the cow flyes bite them so that [they] have no satisfaction so they have put on their shirts and given up," Thomas Lupton wrote home. Thomas wrote again in October, telling folks that the women of the family would not have to cook when the soldiers came home. "[B]oth the boys are cooks of the first class," he wrote, but they were not "fond of the business." Isaac Hite wrote home in November, asking his father to come visit him in camp. He encouraged his father to "bring something to eat, for rations are getting very scarce here. The beef we get for some time is so rank that we can't eat, therefore we have nothing but dry bread."[57]

New recruits continued to dribble into the three companies on station. Between the end of the Gettysburg Campaign and December 31, Company A added fourteen men, Company B added five and Company C gained thirteen troopers. At the same time, Company A had two men declared absent without leave and one a deserter; Company B had several who went absent without leave and two deserters, and Company C had eight men declared absent without leave. Two men died of disease, and eighteen men were sick in a hospital at some point during that time. The men in the company being raised by William Page and John Jackson were not counted.

Not everyone was in favor of Richardson's battalion. In November 1863, Colonel Walter Taylor, a member of General Lee's staff, wrote to his sister about rumors of General Lee losing a horse and of his being unguarded and possibly under the threat of being kidnapped. Lee had not lost a horse, Taylor wrote, and a "battalion of guides & couriers--Gnl Lee's Body Guard as they are pleased to call themselves--the 'Guides, Scouts, Couriers, Detectives and Scamps' as we call them--always attend our Chief's person & never camp more than a mile from him....Don't be alarmed. We aides will shield him from all danger." Taylor, who frequently complained about his workload while serving on Lee's staff, wrote disparagingly of Richardson's battalion. However, he frequently used the couriers for personal correspondence, often encouraging his fiancée to drop off letters at the War Department for speedy delivery.[58]

The year had seen highs and lows. Chancellorsville was a smashing Confederate victory. At the same time, members of the battalion had seen Stonewall Jackson mortally wounded, and the seemingly invincible Confederate army had fought to a draw in the town of Gettysburg. The Thirty-Ninth Battalion had now grown to three companies, and some of their greatest challenges still lay ahead.

Chapter 3

1864

While the winter months often brought a reprieve from active campaigning, the camps near headquarters at Orange Court House were nonetheless busy. Troopers were sent home on furlough and to look for new mounts, new men joined various companies and soldiers were hauled before court-martials for various offenses. Isaac Hite returned to the army from a furlough on January 26. "Since I Came to Camp their [*sic*] has been a strong talk of sending a portion [of] the Batt. back to some place to recruit the horses," he wrote to his sister. Life in the rear, and even away from the army, had its advantages. Forage for horses was more abundant, along with firewood. It was possible for a trooper to slip off for a day or two to visit with nearby family. There was a serious lack of clothing and blankets. Hite wrote that in "order to get any clothing from the government any more, one must lay round in camp mostly naked for a month or two. We had one fellow that had been waring [*sic*] nothing but drawers for some time." Hite was happy to report that clothing was issued on January 26.[59]

"We are fairing [*sic*] pretty well now," Thomas Lupton wrote concerning rations. He and his comrades were getting "three-fourths of a pound of fresh beef per day…half pound corn beef, three and a half pounds of flour and salt," rice, potatoes and lard, along with sugar and "genuine real coffee, none of your confederate compounds." Their horses were getting eight pounds of corn a day, along with a "little hay." The quartermaster was trying to increase the issue to ten pounds of corn a day.[60]

New recruits were still joining the battalion. "Tell all who may ask concerning our Comp. that it is nearly full, and that if they wish to join it, they had better hasten here immediately. We are only allowed a few more. Recruits are coming in every day," Isaac Hite continued his January letter. Company C grew the most in January, with 19 new recruits; 5 were added to Company C in February, and 8 to Company D in March. Overall, the battalion added 52 new members during the first three months of 1864. In January, Lieutenant John Lionberger reported 72 men and 3 officers with Company C on duty at Orange Court House. William Page, with what became part of Company D, had 22 men at Camp Lee. Company A, under Captain Brown, had 58 men at Orange Court House. In February, Captain Page (Company B) reported seventy-three serviceable horses at Orange Court House. Lieutenant Lionberger (Company C) had 3 officers and 72 men present, while William Page (Company D) had thirty-four horses present, and Lieutenant William Green (Company A) reported eighty-two horses. Combined, the battalion had somewhere around 264 men present for duty. Several transferred away from the battalion. Captain William Randolph was relieved of duty on February 24 and apparently sat out the remainder of the war. Corporal John Laws (Company A) died of typhoid in a hospital in Staunton in January, Lieutenant Charles Mount (Company B) was wounded in an undisclosed skirmish in late January and hospitalized in Charlottesville until the end of April, James Franklin (Company B) was detailed as an orderly at Belle Island in early February, Philip Smith (Company B) was discharged for unknown reasons and John Stack (Company D) deserted in late February.[61]

Company D was officially organized in January. Neither Page's detachment nor Lieutenant John Jackson's detachment raised enough men to muster their own companies, and the two were merged to create Company D. This merger had apparently been in the works for some time. Page's appointment as captain was dated January 26, 1864. Jackson's appointment as lieutenant was dated the same day, and it can be assumed this is the date the company was mustered into service. Thomas McKaig Jr., and Robert Temple were also promoted to the rank of lieutenant. Most of the members of Company D had been in service since July and August of the preceding year. Jackson was not pleased about the consolidation, voicing his displeasure in a letter to Robert E. Lee in April.[62]

There were almost a dozen court-martials held during the winter months. When a soldier enlisted, and every time he was mustered to be paid, he was read all 101 Articles of War. These articles governed every soldier—from

The conscript office at Camp Lee in Richmond. Harper's Weekly.

privates to generals. Any infractions were punishable via a court-martial. Those found guilty could lose pay or even be executed. With the army in winter quarters, there was time to look into some of these infractions. Andrew, Godfrey and Siram Stoneberger (Company C) were all tried for theft. Godfrey was found guilty and fined six months' pay. Elijah Broy (Company B) was tried for being absent without leave. Broy was absent from November 1862 until September 1863, when he was arrested and sent to Richmond. He was also found guilty and had his pay stopped. Henry Knight (Company C) was absent for two months between March and April 1863. He was tried for desertion, found guilty and ordered to prison. The same punishment was given to William Taylor (Company C), although it is unclear just when he was absent. James Lines (Company C) was found guilty of violating the fiftieth Article of War: he apparently "quit his guard, platoon, or division." He was fined two months' pay. It was the same crime and punishment for Edward Demaster, also of Company C. James Gentry (Company C) was also charged and convicted of theft. However, his conviction was overturned by President Davis. It seems that Gentry volunteered to help defend Richmond during Sheridan's raid in May 1864, and Davis rewarded him by overturning the conviction. The court-martials were not confined to enlisted men. Lieutenant Andrew Broaddus (Company C) was tried for conduct unbecoming an officer but was acquitted. Albert

Pettigrew (Company C) was tried for violating an order issued by the adjutant and inspector general's office. This order stipulated that officers were not to write to the War Department directly but to go through the official chain of command. A letter had to go to the battalion commander, then whoever was above that person and eventually to Robert E. Lee's office before being forwarded to the War Department. Pettigrew had written to Samuel Cooper on January 13, 1864, regarding conscripts for his company. His trial was on January 27, and his sentence was either remitted or disapproved. Captain Samuel Brown (Company C) was brought up on the charge of "conduct to prejudice good order." He was found guilty and fined. "Captain Brown has been Court Martialed and his centence was read on dress paraid last Wednesday. he is to loose one month's pay. He will be publicky repremanded by Major Richardson," one of Brown's soldiers told the folks back home.[63]

Despite the ramifications of being caught as a deserter, men continued to slip away from the army. Some headed for home, while others headed for Union lines. Holbrook Taylor (Company D) slipped away sometime in late February and headed toward the Federals. According to accounts in Northern newspapers, Private Taylor "was the Orderly of General Lee." While at headquarters, he "forged a dispatch to Gen. Early" and set out. His forged papers allowed him to pass through three different picket posts. Once he was beyond the Confederate lines, he ran into a group of scouts, and pretending "to be lost, would prevail upon them to show him the way." As soon as he was out of sight, he continued to work his way toward Federal lines. Eventually, he was captured and sent to General Meade. After being questioned, he took the oath and was released, stating that he had a brother in Ohio.[64]

Sickness continued to plague many men during the winter months. At least sixteen members of the battalion were reported sick between December 1863 and the end of April 1864. Three had typhoid fever brought on by the contaminated food and water they consumed. Three others had pneumonia, a lung infection. Five of the sixteen who were shipped off to a hospital died of their ailments. Typhoid killed Lieutenant Robert Temple. His mates in Company D wrote a tribute of respect lamenting his death, as they considered Temple a "a gallant officer" who "had won our highest respect." Six of the sixteen were transported to hospitals in Richmond. Others were taken to facilities in Staunton, Orange Court House, Farmville and Gordonsville. Many more undoubtedly fell ill but remained in camp under the care of Assistant Surgeon Marks or their comrades. To help Marks, one of the men was detailed to serve as an apothecary. "He

Left: There were many different Confederate hospitals in Richmond. *Michael C. Hardy.*

Below: Richmond's Chimborazo Hospital was just one of the hospitals where sick members of Lee's Body Guard were sent. *Library of Congress.*

has charge of a meadicens and has to fill out precscriptions. He has been detailed sometime and seems to like it verry well and I think he is a verry good man for the place," one soldier wrote.[65]

A Federal cavalry raid interrupted the doldrums of winter. On February 28, cavalry under Judson Kilpatrick and Ulric Dahlgren crossed over the Rapidan River and headed toward Richmond. As a diversion, George A. Custer led a smaller force on a raid into Albemarle County. On February 29, orders went out to two companies of the battalion to be ready to march at four the next morning. Thomas Lupton wrote of the excursion:

> We started on the first verry early in the morning with the General toward Madison Court House to try and cut off the retreat of a raiding party who crossed on the 28th of February and we marched verry hard to within five miles of Madison when we stoped and made a detail of 10 men to go with Lieutenant Lee on a scout toward the field of action where General Stewart [Stuart] was fighting them on the road from Madison and Stewartsville, and fell to my lot to be one of the detail so we started on the road to Wilftown after about two hours of pretty brisk riding, arrived to a gut in the mountain, were we found a Yank videt station and the Lieutenant thinking that they had a pretty strong reserve thought best not to attack them, so we turned around and went back…to where we overtook the general where we remained untill nearly night when we went back about two miles and camped about three miles from the enemy's lines that night…it rained all day and when we camped, I was so cold and wet I could hardly tie my horse, but we made big fires and dried ourselves, and we were again pretty comfortable.[66]

Custer's raid only lasted until March 1, and he returned to the protection offered by the main Federal army. Both Kilpatrick and Dahlgren failed in their objectives. Kilpatrick was able to hook up with Butler's Federal force near New Kent Court House. Dahlgren's detachment was ambushed, and Dahlgren was killed, with one hundred of his men being captured. Supposedly, found on Dahlgren's body were papers indicating a plot to assassinate President Davis and burn Richmond.

Winter weather continued to harass the soldiers in camp. Franklin Walter (Company A) recorded in his diary that there was snow on March 22, with ten inches by the next morning. "Heavy skirmishing in camp with snow balls," Walter jotted, documenting a common practice among the young soldiers in camp. There was rain and hail on March 25, rain on April 1, rain and snow on April 4, rain the next two days and again on April 9. In a letter home, Walter gave glimpses of the life of a member of the Thirty-Ninth Battalion. Those men whose horses were not serviceable were required to stand guard duty "every other night." At daybreak, or before sunup, the bugle sounded reveille. The troopers formed as the first sergeants called the roll. It was then time to cook breakfast and curry the horses. Those detailed for duty at headquarters were required to be ready at 7:00 a.m. and were not relieved until the next morning. "Some times there is very little to do, and at others, especially when the Yanks make a demonstration, there is a good deal of hard riding for us." Walter believed he rotated on duty every eight days. At nine o'clock, the bugler sounded again, this time for guard mounting. Those not detailed for this twenty-four-hour duty drilled for an hour every morning and afternoon on foot or horseback, weather permitting. Then came time to fix dinner, draw feed for the horses and "attend to our horses." Sometimes, there was a dress parade in the evening and always a final roll call before tattoo was played. "The intervals of leisure moments are taken up by getting wood and water, cleaning up our quarters, brushing up our shoes and in talking, reading, etc." Walter made mention of his mess—five members of his company plus one servant. Since the Confederate government did not allow soldiers to draw rations for their servants, the messmates had to split their rations into six parts.[67]

Slowly, active campaigning started to look more like an immediate possibility. George Koiner (Company C) wrote on March 20 that Lee had all of his lieutenant generals at his headquarters, then at church. "I never saw such a mixture of yellow tape, bars, and stars in my life." Robert E. Lee often met with his generals and government officials in Richmond. He believed that the first real strike that spring would land against the Army of Tennessee, then the Federals would hurl their armies against the Confederate forces in Virginia. In March, U.S. Grant assumed command of all Federal forces. He chose to make his headquarters with the Army of the Potomac, confronting Lee in Virginia. George Meade continued in nominal command. While Longstreet's men had returned from Tennessee, Lee lacked an aggressive commander, like Jackson, who could devise plans to take the war to the enemy. Lee simply waited for Grant and Meade to make the first move.[68]

The first of May brought coordinated attacks across the South. Federal armies were on the move in North Georgia; Mobile, Alabama; and the Shenandoah Valley. The Army of the Potomac, 120,000 men strong, began crossing the Rapidan River on May 4. Companies A, B and C of the Thirty-Ninth Battalion Virginia Cavalry reported 169 men and horses present for duty on May 1. Franklin Walter reported that his company, A, broke camp on May 4, moving toward Verdiersville. On May 5, portions of Grant's army were attacked by Ewell's corps on the Orange Turnpike. That afternoon, Hill's corps engaged other Federal troops on the Orange Plank Road. For many in the Confederate and Union ranks, it was not far from where the two armies had meet a year earlier at Chancellorsville. The area, overgrown and thick with trees and foliage, was aptly named the Wilderness. Any numerically superior force that Grant could boast would be offset by the terrain.

Franklin Walter rotated onto duty as one of Lee's couriers on the morning of May 5. He found the general at a church four miles from Verdiersville. Lee, riding with A.P. Hill and J.E.B. Stuart, along with staffs and couriers, was eleven miles beyond Verdiersville when the group stopped and dismounted in the shade near the Widow Tapp Farm. Suddenly, according to Charles Venable, of Lee's staff, "a party of the enemy's skirmishers deployed from a grove of old-field pines on the left, thus revealing the close proximity of Grant's forces, and the ease of concealing movements in the Wilderness." Walter wrote in his diary that while Lee and Hill "were nearing the front the yanks unexpectedly appeared at the edge of a wood which caused all parties to beat a retreat to the rear of the infantry close by." One of Stuart's aides,

A sketch of General Ewell's 1864 headquarters. Harper's Weekly.

Alexander Boteler, was trying to catch a quick nap when the sound of a horse woke him. He saw "all the generals in full flight from the field followed by their respective aides and couriers…I expected every moment to hear a crashing volley ripping up things around me." Surprisingly, the Federal commander ordered his men to "Right about!" They soon disappeared back into the woods, unmindful of the opportunity they had just missed.[69]

Fighting on May 5 was fierce but inconclusive. The thick woods hampered both sides as they attempted to maneuver. Lee only had two of his three corps in the fight, and by the end of the day, the men on the right were holding their lines but in a disorganized fashion. The general was anxiously awaiting the arrival of Longstreet's corps, who had camped about ten miles to the west. Catlett C. Taliaferro (Company C) was one of the couriers with Lee. During the night, Lee sent Taliaferro to find Longstreet "and urge him to use the utmost diligence in coming to his assistance." Taliaferro rode off into the darkness.

> *I hastened to Gen. Longstreet and delivered the message as given to me, a verbal one, for fear of my capture by the yankees. Gen. Longstreet said: "Go back to Gen. Lee and tell him that I shall be with him at daylight & do anything he wants done." I then remarked, "the yankees are on this road and you had better be careful." He replied, "You be off, sir, and give my message to Gen. Lee; I will take care of any yankees on this road."*

Taliaferro reported back to Lee with the message. The general became convinced, thanks to the urging of generals such as Cadmus Wilcox, that the Federals were poised to attack, and his men were not in a position to receive that attack. Again, Lee sent Taliaferro to find Longstreet. His verbal message was that Longstreet needed to "strain every nerve to reach our lines before day and be in readiness to receive the necessary instructions and make such battle as should be determined on." Taliaferro thought Longstreet "impatient" and ordered him to return to Lee with this message: "Tell him to rest easy; that he would be with him before day and prepared to execute any order he desired."[70]

Federal infantry attacked along the Orange Plank Road just before daylight, pushing parts of Hill's corps to the rear. Confederate soldiers streamed through Lee's headquarters. "Lee became much disturbed and asked, 'Where can Longstreet be? Why had he not come up?'" Taliaferro wrote. He looked down the road and "saw the lead of his column sweeping into view and called the attention of the General to it. Lee directed me to

Robert E. Lee and his generals (from a circa 1864 lithograph by Augustus Tholey). *Library of Congress.*

ride at speed and request Longstreet to bring the men at the double-quick. Longstreet replied: 'Tell Gen. Lee to get on Traveler and ride to the side of the road and let the men see him and all would be well.'" Longstreet stopped to confer with Lee, then led his men forward, stabilizing the line and launching a flank attack.[71]

Longstreet wanted to press his attack. Riding down the Orange Plank Road early that afternoon, Lee's "Old War Horse" was looking for a place to launch the assault. Taliaferro, bearing a message from Lee, had just found Longstreet and his staff when a volley rang out of the woods. Longstreet was shot through the neck and shoulder; General Micah Jenkins was shot in the head and died later that day. Longstreet survived the wound but was unable to serve in the army for months. Many believed, as Taliaferro wrote, that "had Longstreet been up the first day, or had not been wounded even after his long delay, we would have driven Grant across the Rapidan, and ultimately gained our independence." After two days of intense fighting, the battle of the Wilderness ended. Lee stopped Grant's advance. However, instead of retreating back over the river to rest and refit, the Army of the Potomac moved off toward its left flank, heading toward Spotsylvania Court House.[72]

Over three thousand Federal soldiers were captured during the fighting in the Wilderness. Captain Pifer's company was detailed to escort the prisoners to the rear. A member of the Seventy-Sixth New York, John Northrop, captured in the fighting, recalled that their "guard claims to be General Lee's bodyguard: better men than the general run of Rebel soldiers. They grew sociable and easy with us." Another captured soldier was Lieutenant Charles Mattocks, Seventeenth Maine Infantry. Mattocks was captured on May 6 and shuffled off toward prison with the others. He recalled his adventures in his journal:

This morning we started for Orange Court House…We were conducted closely watched, by a detachment of Lee's Body Guard, who were certainly very nice chaps. They showed us every favor possible and even allowed us to ride their horses when we were tired. The sun poured down hot, and the march and heat told on us.…We arrived at Orange Court House at dark, and are now ready to repose upon the steps of the same Hall of Justice. Among the "gentlemen" we have met is Maj. Payden of Lee's Staff, who came along this morning and "raked us down" the office of the guard back of Parker's Store for allowing petty stealing from the prisoners. Captain Pipfer…of Lee's Body Guard, who "escorted" us to Orange Court House, is a very fine gentlemen.[73]

Another of the prisoners was Colonel Walter Harriman, Eleventh New Hampshire Infantry. Harriman stepped away from his regiment and was quietly "taken in" by Confederate pickets. His group of prisoners was escorted to Orange Court House by Lieutenant John Jackson (Company D) of the Thirty-Ninth Battalion. Because he was rather tall, Harriman attracted the attention of Jackson. "Noticing his jaded walk, and that he had passed the prime of life, while we were a mere youth, we called him to the side of the column, dismounted, and had him take our saddle," Jackson later wrote. The conversation between Harriman and Jackson soon turned to who would win the war. Jackson recalled that his

steady and defiant convictions of the triumph of the Union cause and the downfall of the Confederacy is very vivid to-day. We thought it strange at the time that he, the captive, should be so triumphant, instead of despondent, as would have been natural to his age and under his surroundings. We suggested something of the kind, with the additional remarks that we had at least foiled Grant, if not beaten him, and, with further assurance of youth, that the latter was but a matter of a few days' time. Rising to his full length in our short stirrups…for a moment he seemed to think he was again in front of his regiment on the eve of assault, and while his eye flashed, and his hand clutched nervously towards the sabre side, he cried out: "Never! Your success is only ephemeral. God Almighty is back of our army!"[74]

Franklin Walter was on duty May 7 with Lee's headquarters. He made note of riding with Lee "along our lines to the left" and, eventually, to Ewell's headquarters. Grant pushed his army toward the east, but portions of the Confederate army beat him to Spotsylvania Court House, blocking the roads. Lee hurried the rest of his army toward the important crossroads. On May 8, Walter was back in camp when he was ordered to report back to Lee's headquarters. He was cooking and "was compelled to throw away a part of my dough" before he set out to find the commanding general. Walter rode with the headquarters staff as they made their way toward Spotsylvania. Fighting broke out on May 8 as Federals unsuccessfully attempted to push Confederate forces off Laurel Hill. By the next morning, Confederate forces had erected four miles of substantial fortifications around the crossroads. Grant unleashed his cavalry and attempted to smash through the Confederate defenses. Federal cavalry cut Lee's telegraph line. Early on the morning of May 10, Franklin Walter was detailed with seven others of the battalion to form a "relay of couriers from headquarters to Beaver Dam Station." They passed through Spotsylvania Court House and crossed the Po and Mattaponi Rivers before taking their positions. Walter was paired with Lewis Ellis, also of Company A. Their section ran between Walker's store and Wilson's store. Walter recorded that a local citizen brought them coffee, which "stimulated my waning strength very much." About 9:00 p.m., Walter took a message from another courier and rode through the darkness to Wilson's store. He arrived around midnight and passed the message on to Rice Douglass.[75]

Federal attacks created a temporary success on the evening of May 10 as they punched a hole in Confederate lines at Doles's Salient. Catlett Taliaferro (Company C) was again assigned to headquarters staff. He recalled, many years after the war, that when word arrived of the breakthrough, Lee set off to rally the troops and retake the ground. "Members of his staff who were present and other officers, interposed, begging General Lee not to expose himself thus to almost certain death, when he said, 'Then you gentlemen must see that the lines are restored.'" At that moment, Taliaferro wrote,

Col. Walter H. Taylor, the Adjutant-General of his staff, immediately put spurs to his horse, turned toward the fighting line, and I followed him. In a moment we were in the midst of a scene of the greatest excitement and confusion; the Federals held our line of earthworks for a short distance, and were availing themselves of its protection, while firing upon our troops as they advanced to recover the lost ground. A line had been constructed across the base of the triangle...the troops sent to recover the captured position, as they advanced, naturally availed themselves of the protection offered by this new line, and it was a difficult matter to get them to advance beyond it... Col. Taylor, riding in front of the men, cheered on and encouraged them in every way to advance, and finally the line did go forward with a yell and drove the enemy back, retaking the ground and the guns, thus restoring the broken line.

Colonel Taylor had at least one horse shot from underneath him in the action. Taliaferro jumped from his horse to help Taylor and was struck in the arm. "It was the hottest place that I ever was in, and how any escaped has always been a mystery to me," Taliaferro wrote after the war. "All the Staff & couriers that I saw behaved excellent," one staff officer wrote. Another private in the battalion, W.A. Zeaker, was also reported as being wounded, then captured, on May 10.[76]

There was no major combat on May 11, although frequent skirmishes erupted. Early on May 12, Federals again slammed into the Confederate line at the Mule Shoe, breaking the line and driving back the defenders. Fleeing Confederates rallied, and some of the couriers might have helped in the process. Confederates counterattacked, then drove the Federals back over the works, but the fighting stalled into some of the most vicious combat of the entire war. The Federals were on one side of the works, with the Confederates on the other. Overnight, Confederate engineers and infantry finished a line five hundred yards south of the Mule Shoe, and early on the morning of May 13, Confederate forces fell back to the new line. Copious amounts of rainfall sunk both armies in the mud, and operations, save for skirmishing, became bogged down as well. There was another Federal assault on May 18 that did nothing but add to Federal losses. On the night of May 20 and the early morning of May 21, Grant again moved to the east and south in an attempt to get between the Confederate army and Richmond. Losses were over eighteen thousand Federals and twelve thousand Confederates. Besides Taliaferro and Zeaker, the Thirty-Ninth Battalion lost John Beltcher (Company D), who was captured on May 15.[77]

Franklin Walter had a chance to ride over the battlefield on May 20. He saw many of the Federal unburied "in an advanced state of decomposition and the stench was unbearable." In a section of woods, Walter could mark the lines of the enemy by where their dead lay. The "trees were perfectly riddled with musket balls; many trees being cut off by solid shot and shell. The mark of musket balls on the trees showed remarkably accurate firing, very few being higher than a man." Walter rode on, picking up a few things he needed from the debris of war scattered on the ground.[78]

Lee began moving his army east on May 21. Once again, Grant was trying to get between him and Richmond. The Thirty-Ninth Battalion broke camp at 10:00 a.m. Some four hundred Federal prisoners traveled in front of the battalion as they moved along. Among the Federals captured at Spotsylvania was Joseph Ferguson, an officer in the First New Jersey Infantry. While Ferguson's comrades captured during the Wilderness had positive observations about their treatment at the hands of the Thirty-Ninth Battalion, he believed that "a more dastardly organization of robbers never sat on horses. They watched every opportunity to goad, taunt, steal from and maltreat the unfortunates in their charge. With a Quixotic air they would sneeringly ask us, 'Will you take a ride?'" Ferguson told of a "light-haired boy" with whom he had shared a cracker stumbling and being struck by a saber. His own hat was stolen one night as he slept, and others lost their shoes. The battalion went into camp near the Po River, where they received mail for the first time in months.[79]

On the morning of May 22, Lee again beat Grant. Confederate forces began constructing works at Hanover Junction along the North Anna River. To cross the river and engage the Federals, Grant would have to divide his army. On May 23, Federal troops crossed at Jericho Mills and the Chesterfield bridge. Thinking that the Confederates were retreating, the Federals advanced on May 24. Eventually, they ran into strong Confederate entrenchments, and after several futile attacks, the Federals disengaged.

Parts of the battalion not escorting prisoners throughout May 21 and 22 were with the army. On the evening of May 22, they went into camp one and a half miles south of Hanover Junction, where they bathed, possibly for the first time since the campaign commenced. Some members of the battalion were ordered to report to Major General Martin Smith, the Army of Northern Virginia's chief engineer. Franklin Walter recalled riding with Smith from the North Anna River "telegraph bridge all along the course of the river before selecting positions for our guns." They then returned to headquarters and were ordered to A.P. Hill's headquarters at Anderson's Turnout. Hill sent word back to Lee, through Franklin Walter, that "the enemy had crossed the river in considerable force on our left" and that Hill wanted "reinforcements in order to attack and drive them back." Walter rode back, seeking Lee or Ewell for help for General Hill. On returning to the river, the "yanks being in sight on the other side," Walter was under fire, "some of their shells bursting near us." That evening, Walter reported that his horse was "considerable jaded by the hard days riding."[80]

About this time, Thomas Lupton noted a change in operations: "We now send a Lieutenant with couriers from headquarters." This was apparently a new procedure, and, possibly, in the past, courier details were sent only with noncommissioned officers. Lupton noted that Lieutenant George Balthorpe was on duty and sent with a verbal order to Major General Richard R. Anderson. In the course of the ride, Balthorpe was apparently struck in the arm by a shell fragment but "did not leave the field." Lupton recalled that he himself was exposed "to some pretty heavy shelling," with one of those shells "striking the ground so close to me and exploded that it threw dirt all over me." A member of Lee's staff, Colonel Charles Marshall, "was slightly wounded above the eye and knocked the glass out of his spectacles."[81]

The battle of North Anna River came to an end on May 27. Grant once again began shifting his forces southeast in an attempt to get between Lee and Richmond. The Thirty-Ninth Battalion was up and on the road by 9:00 a.m. Portions of the battalion trailed behind an ailing Lee as he rambled along in his carriage. There was a halt at Ashland to graze their horses. They were in the saddle soon thereafter and did not halt until two the next morning. Lee made his headquarters at the Jenkins house just off the Telegraph Road and not far from the road to Atlee's. On May 28, after ordering cavalry to probe the roads in the area, Lee moved his headquarters to Lockwood, the home of the Clarke family. He had been ill for some days, possibly from drinking contaminated buttermilk, and did not leave the home for a couple of days. General Ewell was also unwell. He was forced to turn command over to Jubal Early and headed for Richmond. The commander who had recruited the original company of the Thirty-Ninth Battalion would not return. At the end of May 1864, Captain Pifer reported eighty horses present in Company A, sixty-nine horses under Captain Brown in Company C and sixty-one horses under Captain Page in Company D.[82]

Major General Jubal Early took over command of the Second Corps after Richard Ewell's reassignment. *Library of Congress.*

Lee's illness kept him from riding the lines as he had done in so many campaigns. Walter Taylor, on Lee's staff, noted that Lee "remained more quiet & directs movements from a distance." Colonel Taylor was writing on June 1 and noted that all of the staff were delivering messages save himself. This undoubtedly meant more work for the Thirty-Ninth Battalion. There were Federal attacks near Cold Harbor that broke through the Confederate lines. Counterattacks drove back the Federals. James Boswell (Company C) was captured on June 1. Grant planned to renew the attack on June 2, but his reinforcements failed to get into position. It was a gift to the Confederates, as they used the time to strengthen their works. Federals launched attacks early on the morning of June 3. Thomas Lupton was not on duty but talked to members of the battalion working under Major General Robert F. Hoke, who had just transferred to Lee's army a few days before. The attack had begun early, he wrote, and continued to midday, when the Federals "gave it up as a bad gain." It was Lupton's guess that seven different assaults were made against Confederate entrenchments "but were repulsed each time with frightful loss. The ground being literally covered with their dead and wounded." His fellow troopers told him that "they could walk for a hundred yard on Yankees without touching the ground." A captured officer held near Lupton's camp told the courier that "he had been in the war ever since 61 and that he had never seen such a slaughter in his life, and that the army was verry much dissatisfied with Grant in having the men slaughtered up in the way they were."[83]

Lupton went on to detail his experience during the campaign to date.

It has been a verry hard campaign on both men and horses. The hardest that I have ever been on. For the first sixteen days...[I] had but three days rest out of the saddle and four days my horse had nothing to eat. I was on duty at that time as a realai [relay] courier from Chesterfield Station on the central railroad and on the fourth day I started to headquarters with some dispaches and when I got to the place where headquarters had been, I found them gone and my horse was so compleatly exhausted from hunger and hard ridding, I had to leave him in an old stable and I took my blanket and overcoat and started on foot for headquarters a distance of about 2 1/2 miles, where I delivered my dispatches and started back for my horse, which I found rested some. I then fixed up and started on in pursuit of my company, which had gone on toward Hanover Junction, where I overtook our commissary Sgt, with one of the wagons loaded with rations and some corn and I concluded to stay with him until I found my battalion. My horse has not been able to do much duty since, but he is improving and will soon be able to do duty again.[84]

Grant's army had suffered a serious blow at the battle of Cold Harbor. Federal losses in just one hour on June 3 were estimated at seven thousand men, with another five thousand killed, wounded and captured on June 1 and 2. The two armies were left eyeing each other across the battle-torn landscape.

For a few days, while Grant planned his next move, the war shifted elsewhere. In the Shenandoah Valley, Federal forces under General David Hunter swept into Staunton on June 5. "Received the news of the occupation of Staunton by the enemy," Franklin Walter jotted in his diary on June 7. Staunton had served at a Confederate headquarters, a depot, a commissary, a quartermaster post and a training camp for two years. Hunter's forces looted food and valuables from local citizens, then set fire to the railroad depot, warehouses, mills, factories and stores. Many members of the battalion came from the Shenandoah Valley and had family back at home trying to survive. However, there is no noticeable uptick of men absent without leave in the month of June.[85]

On June 6, Grant finally called for a truce to bury the dead and care for the wounded. Federal parties arrived the following day for the grisly work. Most of the wounded Federals left on the field had perished by this time. Lee was frequently seen riding along the lines, inspecting his own positions and always looking for an opportunity to strike. Johnson Hagood, whose brigade had recently transferred from South Carolina, recalled seeing Lee after the battle of Cold Harbor. An orderly, possibly a member of the Thirty-Ninth Battalion, was standing not far from Lee's tent holding the reins of the general's horse. Lee "wore blue military pants without suspenders and short linen sack with no vest, a soft felt hat, and buff gauntlets. He had no insignia of rank about him, and carried neither sword, pistol or field glass." After a moment, Lee mounted the horse "and rode quietly away followed by the orderly. This was his usual style."[86]

Federal forces under General Benjamin Butler attacked Petersburg on June 9. The attacks were poorly coordinated, and Confederate forces still held the city at the end of the day. Lee was uncertain about the intentions of the Federal army. Parts of the Thirty-Ninth Battalion spent the day corralling prisoners and guarding fields of oats and rye. Grant began moving the Army of the Potomac across the James River, toward the Petersburg defenses, on June 12. Lee began to shift the Army of Northern Virginia toward the Long Bridge area of the Chickahominy River, unconvinced that Grant's true objective was Petersburg. The Thirty-Ninth Battalion broke camp early on the afternoon of June 13, crossing the Chickahominy and eventually going into camp about four miles from Malvern Hill on the Charles City Road. The men were undoubtedly hungry. The day before, they had given their day's rations to Southern refugees passing through the Confederate lines. There was another attack on Petersburg on June 15— one that almost succeeded. But, mixed Federal orders and courageous Confederate defenders kept the Federals from taking the Cockade City. Lee still believed the Army of the Potomac to be located north of the James River, and cries for reinforcements fell on deaf ears. Almost all of the Army of the Potomac was south of the James River by June 16. An attack on the Petersburg defenses east of the city punched through the lines, and another attack captured Bermuda Hundred. Two divisions of Lee's army were sent to Bermuda Hundred and recaptured the works that evening. The Thirty-Ninth Battalion broke camp that morning, going into camp near Drewry's Bluff. "General Lee crossed the river today," Walter wrote, "and tonight his headquarters are on the south side of the James." It was not only Lee who crossed the river; two Confederate corps were on their way as well.[87]

Lee pitched his headquarters tents on the Shippen family estate, called Violet Bank, not far from the Appomattox River. According to Walter Taylor, Lee was "offered a room for" his use, while the "tents were pitched in the yard." However, the campsite was exposed to Federal artillery fire as the war progressed.[88]

Portions of the Thirty-Ninth Battalion broke camp and crossed the James River on June 18. Their present camp was on the Richmond and Petersburg Turnpike, about a half-mile from Petersburg and south of the Appomattox River. Lee's couriers were obviously busy. William Childress (Company C) was captured around June 15, Benjamin Conrad (Company A) was wounded

25—General Lee Headquarters, Petersburg, Va.

Petersburg's Violet Bank, constructed in 1815, served as Lee's headquarters from June through November 1864. *Michael C. Hardy.*

and sent to the hospital in Gordonville and James Bowles (Company D) was wounded in the left wrist and sent to a Richmond hospital on June 20. On June 21, Captain Pifer reported eighty horses available for duty in Company A, while Captain Brown reported sixty-seven horses in Company C. Nine days later, Lieutenant Thomas McKaig reported fifty-four serviceable horses for Company D, while Lieutenant Thomas Turner, Company B, reported twenty-nine horses for his company.[89]

There is little information about the battalion during the month of July 1864. "The position of the two armies around Petersburg is yet the same," Isaac Hite (Company C) wrote home. "Picket firing is yet kept up nearly constantly." Troopers rotated on and off duty on a regular basis. Franklin Walter wrote that an artillery shell landed in the camp of Company C on July 6, exploding and severely wounding a horse but striking no people. Toward the end of the month, Hite noted that the artillery firing into the city had been reduced to mortars. "They are very beautiful to look at," he wrote. "They are shot high in the air, making the arc of a circle, so that they will drop just behind the fortif[i]cations and explode." It is possible that some members of the battalion went with Early's Corps into the Shenandoah Valley. Three members of the battalion—Beverly Codwise, William Gibbon and James Kinnier—were all captured while "on a scout" on July 9 between Martinsburg and Hedgeville, West Virginia. Codwise and Kinnier were members of Company C, while Gibbon was a trooper in Company D. Randolph Ridgeley, a former member of Company B but then serving on the staff of General Stephen D. Ramseur, was wounded in the thigh on July 20 at the battle of Rutherford's Farm. Ridgeley originally enlisted in the Thirty-Ninth Battalion in November 1862 and, based upon a recommendation by Henry Kyd Douglas of Jackson's staff, was detailed as a courier to Jackson's staff, then as an aide-de-camp to Jubal Early. When Early was promoted to corps command, Ridgeley remained behind on division staff. During the battle, Ridgeley was ordered to ride to the left to inform the officers their left was being turned by the Federals. The Confederate line broke about the time Ridgeley arrived. He was then wounded and left on the field. That evening, Douglas, who had witnessed Ridgeley's fall, asked one of the ladies in Winchester to seek out Ridgeley. She did so and saved the young soldier's life.[90]

Henry Cooper (Company A) penned a letter to a friend back home on July 17, giving a glimpse at the experiences shared by many in the Army of Northern Virginia. "I am getting tired of camp life," Cooper wrote. He considered Grant "the worst whipped general that has tried to take Richmond.…There has been more Yankees killed than in any other fight. I got sick of seeing dead Yankees. Grant has [a] strong position in front of Petersburg but when his men come out of their breastworks, our men will slay them as same as they did at Cold Harbor."[91]

Several members of the battalion were reported sick in this period of time, mostly with dysentery or chronic diarrhea. Two members of the battalion deserted. Franklin Walter wrote about returning to camp on July 19 from a rotation at army headquarters only to find his clothing gone. He also commented on the July 30 attack below Petersburg, where Federals blew up a portion of the Confederate line from an underground mine, then sent soldiers into the pit. "Our forces drove them out. Killing 700, recapturing our guns and taking from the enemy 20 stand of colors and a goodly number of prisoners, amongst them about 200 negroes." It is unclear if Walter witnessed the battle of the Crater or was simply relating what others had heard or told him.[92]

Three of the companies provided returns the first of August. Company A reported sixty-five horses present and able for duty, Company C reported fifty-nine and Company D reported forty-three. Confederate and Federal troops continued to watch each other in and around Petersburg. Grant was continually trying to cut all lines of communication and supply from the south into Petersburg. One Federal corps attacked the Weldon Railroad on August 18. Confederates counterattacked, and while they won the tactical victory, the Federals still held the railroad, forcing Confederates to disembark supplies twelve miles to the south. The August 25 fight was known as the battle of Reams Station. The only loss the Thirty-Ninth Battalion reported for the month was John Skidmore (Company D), who was captured near Falls Church and initially sent to Old Capitol Prison in Washington, and then on to Elmira in New York.[93]

At the end of August, Edmund Jones (Company C) was assigned as a clerk at army headquarters. At least four others—William Ward (Company A), James Denny (Company A), Marion Hite (Company C) and Joshua Thomas (Company D)—also served as clerks at Army of Northern Virginia headquarters. Many viewed the job as mundane. Clerks handled the copious amount of documents coming in and going out and copied orders or other missives. Colonel Walter Taylor, of Lee's staff, wrote in January 1864 that he employed five soldiers as clerks and needed another. There were undoubtedly many others who might have served as clerks at the corps or division level, but only two were listed. William Lithgown (Company B) was detailed as a clerk in the Confederate Ambulance Works in Richmond, while William Littlejohn (Company B) worked in the inspector's office.[94]

With longer periods of time between battles, the Thirty-Ninth could attend to battalion business. Eight troopers were hauled before the officers and tried for some unknown offenses. Seven men were fined one month's pay, while the other was fined two months' pay. Three companies reported how many horses were present and able to do duty on September 1; Company A reported sixty-seven horses, Company B twenty-seven horses and Company D forty-one horses. However, many men were parceled out to various headquarters, and their mounts might not have been included in those numbers. James Bowles (Company D) was assigned to Major General Robert F. Hoke's command; Richard Jacobs (Company D) was with Early's Corps; William Jenkins was detailed to support Lieutenant General A.P. Hill; and Sergeant Charles Forsyth, at least for the week of September 12–19, was reported to be attached with eleven men at Major General George Pickett's division. A few other men were detailed to posts. Henry Mohler (Company C) was stationed at Drewry's Bluff; Patrick Murphy (Company D) served hospitals in Lynchburg; Charles Sloat (Company A) worked as a carpenter at the quartermaster's depot; and Richard Shacklett (Company A) served in the quartermaster's department in Columbia, South Carolina.[95]

Several members of Lee's Body Guard were reportedly assigned to the command of Major General George Pickett. Harper's Weekly.

Lieutenant George Balthorpe (Company A) submitted his resignation on September 8. He stated that he desired to see more active service and wanted to join another cavalry command. Major Richardson forwarded Balthorpe's request, believing that Balthorpe was "not an efficient officer." Balthorpe went on to serve as a private in Mosby's Forty-Third Battalion Virginia Cavalry. Several other men were lost from the Thirty-Ninth in the month of September. Typhoid fever killed Samuel Wood (Company D) in Chimborazo Hospital in Richmond on September 11. The same illness felled James Boswell (Company C) at the prison camp in Elmira, New York. Fifteen other members of the battalion were reported sick, most with some type of fever or chronic diarrhea. Five others were declared absent without leave.[96]

While R.R. Stringfellow (Company B) was wounded in the left foot on September 1, most of the fighting in September came later in the month. George Coiner (Company C) wrote home on September 1 about the continual shelling the troops had to endure. "The shells are falling thick & fast in the poor old city," he wrote from Petersburg. Since taking up his pen, a shell had landed "not 150 [yards] from my tent....They have thrown several right in our camp." Franklin Walter wrote home on September 7. He had recently been on leave. Walter complained that the battalion was "doing more duty now than it has ever done before." When not on courier duty, the men were on guard duty. However, "although some of us sometime complain of the amount of duty we have to do, yet we all congratulate ourselves that we are in a much easier place than in regular cavalry beside being less exposed to the pellets of the enemy." Walter goes on, stating that that the couriers were now on duty "seven days at a time" and were required to stand guard at Lee's tent for five hours during that time. In the Shenandoah Valley, the third battle of Winchester was fought on September 19. The Federals simply overpowered Jubal Early's command that day and again on September 22 at Fisher's Hill. On the Petersburg-Richmond front, Federals launched an effort to extend their lines, working toward the Southside Railroad and the Appomattox River. Federal attacks overran Fort Archer, and Confederate counterattacks on September 29 and October 1 failed to dislodge their foes. Federal entrenchments were extended from the Weldon Railroad west to Pegram's Farm. There was also an attack north of the James River at Chaffin's Bluff, and again, the Confederates were forced back and compelled to erect new fortifications.[97]

Toward the end of September, Franklin Walter was assigned to duty at a signal station near General Pickett's headquarters. There were probably others assigned to such duty throughout the battalion and over the course of the war. The men assigned to the signal corps observed the enemy and passed messages, sometimes using flags in the daytime and torches at night. Walter's job was probably still that of a courier. When a message arrived or intelligence about enemy movements was received, Walter could have relayed this information to surrounding commanders. He reported being on duty at the station from September 26 to October 3 and again from October 10 until an unknown date.[98]

It would appear that Lieutenant Thomas Turner and Company B were redeployed to Gordonsville toward the end of September. They undoubtedly were there to serve as a link between the Confederates in the Shenandoah Valley and the War Department in Richmond. Turner reported that he had forty horses present for duty. Several members of the Thirty-Ninth Battalion were wounded during the following month. James Finn (Company B) was wounded on an undisclosed date and admitted to a hospital in Charlottesville. Austin Myers (Company C) was wounded and captured at Beverly on October 29. He spent the rest of the war at the Camp Chase and Point Lookout prisoner camps. Corporal Henry Tongue was captured on October 6, and Lewis Weaver was captured October 9, both at Rapidan Station. Both were members of Company B, and both were sent to Point Lookout. David Middleton (Company C) was captured in Strasburg on October 19 and sent to West Building Hospital in Baltimore. Given the option, Middleton took the oath of allegiance in February 1865 and was released. Six members of the battalion were reported sick and admitted to various hospitals. Two members of the battalion were reported absent without leave, while James Brander (Company D) died of chronic diarrhea while imprisoned at Elmira, New York.[99]

General Longstreet returned to the command of his corps on October 17 after recovering from his wound received at the Wilderness. A couple of days later, the last major engagement in the Shenandoah Valley was fought. "Your last letter almost sickens me to think how mien the cowardly yankees have done," a Thirty-Ninth soldier from the valley wrote. "I[t] would seem like enough to provoke the Heavens to wrathful vengeance, and change every spring of grass to venomous adders to sting the villains to destruction." The Confederates achieved early success at Cedar Creek, but the timely arrival of the Union commander changed the battle to a Federal victory. On the Richmond-Petersburg front, there were battles at Hatcher's Run and Burgess Mill. Information about the wide-ranging war undoubtedly filtered down from the top to the couriers, scouts and guides. Isaac Hite had written home a few months earlier, "[P]ease seemed quite favorable....Then came the fall of Atlanta with some other reverses to our arms which soon settled the dark cloud on our side." Hite thought that Grant's failures to capture certain positions were again changing the winds of war, and he hoped the losses incurred in the campaigns of 1864 would bear witness in the upcoming Northern elections. For the South to win the war, Hite believed that "we will have to do away with slavery—renounce self government, and call on England or France to aid us to established a limited mona[r]chy." He noted that Richmond newspaper editors were in favor of granting slaves freedom if they would join the Southern armies. "But this I do not believe would do us any good. If northern negroes will not fight who have been enlightened and permitted to enjoy many privileges, It is not reasonable to suppose that a Southern field negro will....Besides if this is a white man's government let white men sustain it or let it fall."[100]

The shortage of horseflesh became apparent in November and December 1864. While two soldiers had been sent home on "horse detail" in October, additional troopers were sent to look for new mounts. In November, five members of Company D were sent out. In December, fifteen troopers were sent out: five from Company A, five from Company C, four from Company D and one from Company B.

"Lee moved Hqs. to Petersburg," Franklin Walter wrote on November 1. Apparently, the loss of summer foliage exposed Violet Bank to Federal observers and artillery. In November, Lee shifted his headquarters from Violet Bank to the Beasley Home on High Street in the west end of Petersburg. For the next month, the house served as the headquarters of the Army of Northern Virginia. "This is the first time we have been quartered in a house," Colonel Walter Taylor wrote. At the end of the month, Lee again shifted his headquarters a couple miles to the west, to Edge Hill, the home of the Turnbull family. "I am finely fixed in the parlor with piano, sofas, rocking-chairs, and pictures; capital surroundings for a winter campaign," Taylor wrote. On November 24, George Coiner (Company C) returned to camp from leave. The battalion's camp was not far from headquarters. He found his comrades building winter quarters.[101]

When Lee moved his headquarters from Violet Bank to the Beasley house, Franklin Walter wrote that he and Robert Campbell were left behind at the telegraph office. Edward Walton (Company D) also recalled that he served at the telegraph office in Petersburg. There were regular, usually civilian, telegraph operators at the station in Petersburg and elsewhere. Those detailed to the office were given messages coming in over the wire and would then deliver those messages to army headquarters. Couriers worked under all conditions. Colonel Walter Taylor reported in December that couriers were arriving all throughout the night, "and what a bitter cold night it was!" Couriers had to ride in the cold, snow, rain and mud as well as the blistering, dusty heat of summer.[102]

Troopers continued to slip away from the Thirty-Ninth. Three members of the battalion left in November, and four left in December. Desertion was an epidemic plaguing the entire Army of Northern Virginia. During the

The remnants of Edge Hill, Lee's Petersburg headquarters, after the evacuation of Petersburg. *Library of Congress.*

same period, ten members of the battalion were reported sick at various hospitals. On December 10, Isaac Hite wrote home for the last time in 1864. Portions of his letter are insightful regarding the conditions the men and horses were forced to endure. The battalion's horses were not drawing any corn and were only given a little hay. "They will all die before spring with this," Hite concluded. He advised those back at home to sell any horses they had, believing the government would impress what was available in the spring. George Coiner echoed Hite regarding horseflesh. He found his company's horses "looking very badly Don't get any long food at all now. Get oats - & these are not much account." Hite also complained that many of the soldiers were "very mien [mean]." Lack of food forced the men into gangs "of six to a dozen" who went "through the country and do just as they please." The local population feared these gangs. "They shoot down stock, break into their meet houses, and take any thing that they want…they frequently shoot" owners trying to defend their property. In one instance, these gangs had killed a child while aiming at a lady scolding them about taking property. "It is awful! Can a just God behold such iniquity much longer. I think it is alarming to see how fast this government is going to ruin," Hite wrote. "I fear we will never be a free people again."[103]

Fighting largely shifted away from Virginia in the last two months of 1864. In Georgia, Federal armies began their march to the sea. Confederate forces headed in the opposite direction, trying to draw back the Federals. The battles of Franklin and Nashville, Tennessee, in November and December, respectively, wrecked the Confederate Army of Tennessee, along with whatever slim chances Southerners held out for independence. Overall, 1864 had been a trying year for members of the Thirty-Ninth Battalion Virginia Cavalry. Campaigning during the spring and summer months went on unabated, and as the year ended, Confederate forces were struggling to hold two of their most important cities: Petersburg and Richmond.

Chapter 4

1865

Every two months, according to Confederate regulation, the members of the Thirty-Ninth Battalion Virginia Cavalry should have been mustered to be paid. Company officers would labor over the sheets, writing down the names of the men who were present, absent on furlough, absent without leave or in the hospital. Soldiers who owed the government money for lost or damaged equipment had the sums deducted from their pay. Privates in the cavalry in 1863 received $12 per month—a dollar more than their infantry cohorts. Also, since most of the mounted men furnished their own horses, troopers received a forage allowance. A captain of a cavalry company received $140 per month plus a forage allowance for three horses. These records are the primary sources of information about the lives of the troopers. However, the last remaining muster roll for the Thirty-Ninth Battalion appears to be the one for December 1864. The battalion's records for the next four months do not appear to have survived.

The bitter cold of winter slowed the war that was being waged in Virginia. "Many of our friends and neighbors who greeted last New Year's day are now slumbering beneath the clods of Virginia's battlefields," George Coiner wrote home on January 2. "Other[s] only live to see the new year from [a] loathsome Yankee prison." Federal soldiers manning the Bermuda Hundred line were shipped south for a new expedition against Fort Fisher, which was below Wilmington, North Carolina. On January 13, the attack on Fort Fisher began, and the fort fell to a combined naval and infantry attack the next day. On January 17, the Federal army that had captured Savannah began moving north toward Columbia, South Carolina. On January 23, Lee was appointed general-in-chief of all Confederate armies. It was undoubtedly too little, too late, and nothing indicates an uptick in the workload of the Thirty-Ninth Battalion. Instead, the men were busy constructing stables for their horses and complaining about the scarcity of rations they were receiving.[104]

On January 24, prisoner exchanges began again. Policy breakdowns, largely over the disposition of captured members of the U.S. Colored Troops, had brought the exchange of prisoners to a halt in mid-1863. Prison populations soared, and exposure and disease, coupled with inadequate rations, killed thousands. It was not until early March that the first soldiers started returning to the South. At least forty-eight members of the Thirty-Ninth Battalion were captured and incarcerated during the war years. Six troopers died while they were imprisoned. One other chose to take the oath of allegiance and join the U.S. Army. At least two took the oath and were released north of the Mason-Dixon line. John Miller (Company A) deserted to the enemy and was sent to Fort Mifflin in Pennsylvania but later escaped. Only six members of the battalion had been released by the end of March.[105]

February was cold for the couriers and scouts of the Thirty-Ninth Battalion. Early that month was the battle of Hatcher's Run. Grant continued to push west, stretching Confederate defenses. There was little Lee could do. The Federal army in South Carolina continued to move toward Columbia. A battle was fought at Aiken on February 11 and resulted in a small Confederate victory. Yet Columbia fell on February 17, and much of the city was left in ashes. After leaving Columbia, the Federals headed toward Fayetteville, North Carolina. Within the battalion, George Russell (Company A) was admitted to a Richmond hospital with either a wounded foot or sprained ankle. Thomas Smith (Company B) was court-martialed on February 23 for disobedience of orders, but he was acquitted.[106]

Two members of the Thirty-Ninth Battalion were captured on March 7. William Ray and James Lupton, both members of Company A, were scouting near Cedar Creek when they were picked up by Federal cavalry. Both were labeled as guerrillas and sent to Fort McHenry. Attached to both files was an annotation: "Not to be exchanged during the war. By order of Maj. Gen. Sheridan." Being captured and labeled a guerrilla was a dangerous business. A guerrilla engaged in nonconventional warfare, often ambushing regular soldiers, capturing supplies and, at times, raiding civilians. In some instances, captured guerrillas were executed on the spot. Both Lupton and

Ray survived the war, making them more fortunate than many others who were labeled guerrillas.[107]

On March 8, James Warder (Company A) deserted to the enemy. Warder had joined in October 1863 but had first deserted in December 1864. It is possible he hid out until crossing over into Union lines at Alexandria on March 8. He claimed that he was "opposed to [the] war." On March 20, Warder took the oath of allegiance and was sent to New Jersey. The previous January, Grant had promised deserters food and free transportation if their homes were within the lines. Or, a deserter might be able to obtain a job in the army in one of the various departments as a laborer once he took the oath of allegiance. If deserters brought their rifles with them, they were paid for those, as well. Between January 10 and March 28, Lee's army lost at least 5,928 to desertion.[108]

As the final days of the Army of Northern Virginia played out, there were changes in the command of the Thirty-Ninth Battalion Virginia Cavalry. Major Richardson last appears in the records on February 25, when there was an issue of clothing. Captain Pifer was reported as in command of the battalion in late 1864, on detail in January 1865 and then as being relieved of command of Company A for unknown reasons on March 17. Captain William Page is last reported in the records of Company D in November– December 1864, when he is recorded as absent on leave. Command of the battalion seems to have fallen upon the shoulders of Captain Samuel Brown (Company C). There was widespread fighting in North Carolina at places like Kinston, Averasborough and Bentonville. In Virginia, there were skirmishes in the Shenandoah Valley and naval operations up the Rappahannock River.[109]

On March 25, Lee cobbled together a force and attacked the Federal position at Fort Stedman east of Petersburg. He hoped to force Grant to contract his Federal lines. Confederates quickly overwhelmed the fort and surrounding entrenchments but lacked the numbers to hold their gains. Federal counterattacks drove the Confederates back to their own trenches. Dejected, Lee wrote to Jefferson Davis: "I fear now it will be impossible to prevent a junction between Grant and Sherman, nor do I deem it prudent that this army should maintain its position until the latter shall approach too near." On March 29, Grant began to move on Lee and the Confederate defenses surrounding Petersburg and Richmond. Lee again cobbled together a force under George Pickett and Fitzhugh Lee and sent them to the west, toward Five Forks. There was skirmishing over the last three days of March. Lee told Pickett to "Hold

William Jenkins was with Lieutenant General A.P. Hill as Hill rode toward Confederate lines. *Library of Congress.*

Five Forks at all hazards," a note that was probably delivered by a courier from the Thirty-Ninth Battalion. Confederate defenses around Five Forks crumbled under a Federal attack late on the afternoon of April 1. The Federal army almost completely surrounded the Confederate defenders. Lee informed Davis that to save the army, the evacuation of Petersburg and Richmond would be necessary; since Edward Walter (Company D) served as a relay between Lee's headquarters and the telegraph office in Petersburg, it is possible that he carried this message from Lee.[110]

William Jenkins (Company C) was on duty the night of April 1 at A.P. Hill's headquarters. During the night, Jenkins was called upon to deliver some papers from Hill to Lee and then to Heth. "I saw the General was troubled," Jenkins wrote of Lee. As Jenkins turned to head toward Heth's headquarters, Lee gave a message to relay to Heth: "Jenkins, tell Gen. Heth, for me, to keep a close watch on the enemy's movements, and report every move to me at once." The courier then rode off into the darkness.[111]

Under the cover of darkness, Grant massed Federal troops outside the Confederate works below Petersburg. Lee had pulled ten thousand troops out of the entrenchments and sent them to Five Forks. One Tar Heel soldier recalled that he and his comrades were spread ten paces apart behind the works. Before daylight, those massed Federals punched a hole in the Confederate line, working their way to the right and left and capturing hundreds of Confederate soldiers.[112]

Lee's headquarters at Edge Hill were roughly two miles from where the breakthrough occurred. During the early morning hours, A.P. Hill and James Longstreet arrived at Edge Hill to confer with Lee. As they talked, a staff officer burst into the room with news that wagons and teamsters were fleeing down a nearby road, and the Federals were reportedly just a half-mile away. Hill quickly mounted his horse and rode off to the right with two couriers, Sergeant George W. Tucker and William Jenkins, who had arrived from Heth's headquarters, in an effort to gain information and rally his troops. "We then proceeded on our way to the westward," Jenkins wrote over thirty years after the war. "We had gone probably about a mile when we came upon two bluecoats (stragglers), whom we disarmed." Hill ordered Jenkins to take the two prisoners back to Lee's headquarters.

> *I immediately started back with the prisoners, but had not gone more than half a mile when I encountered a squad of 12 to 15 armed infantrymen near a peach orchard, west of the Venable House. I at once dismissed my prisoners, and falling flat on my horse's back, ran the gauntlet.*
>
> *These men had crossed the road, gone north, and were returning. When they saw me they commenced firing and as they were not more than 200 yards away I made the run through the peach orchard under this fire and at the east end of the orchard I got out of their range, as I went down an incline which hid me from the firing squad. Then I proceeded on my way to Lee's headquarters, and when I got there Serg't Tucker had just arrived with the General's horse and his own.*

General Hill and Tucker continued toward the right after Jenkins left and headed toward Edge Hill with his prisoners. The pair soon came upon two Federal soldiers and demanded their surrender. Instead of throwing down their arms, the Federals fired, killing the general. Tucker caught his horse and quickly rode away, bearing the mournful news to Lee. "Gen. Hill's death caused a wave of great sorrow all thru the army," Jenkins recalled.[113]

Portions of the Confederate army fell back into the inner works. Heroic stands by small numbers of Confederates at Batteries Gregg and Wentworth allowed Lee to hold on until nightfall. In Richmond, Davis had received word that the lines could no longer be sustained. Davis, the cabinet and many government employees piled onto the trains and headed west toward Danville. Under the cover of darkness, Lee pulled his army out of the Petersburg trenches. "I was roused up from sleep about 11 o'clock last night and told that the lines from Chaffin['s] to Richmond were being evacuated," Franklin Walter recorded in his diary. He wrote of the destruction of the fortifications at Chaffin's and Drewry's Bluff that night. Near daybreak, they were crossing at the Rocketts on the James River and witnessed the gunboats and naval stores going up in flames. "Crossed Mayo's bridge one hour after sunrise. A large tobacco warehouse was burning when we crossed. Mayo's bridge was burnt a few minutes after we crossed."[114]

Lee's army moved west toward Amelia Court House on April 3. Siram Stoneberger (Company C) was scooped up by the Federals in Petersburg and sent as a prisoner to Hart's Island. Franklin Walter was moving along with the retreating column—apparently not with Lee or the headquarters staff. On April 4, he reported that he "rode to Brookhill farm on the Gurney road about 50 miles from Richmond" and camped at "Mr. Brightwell." The next day, they started toward Farmville, but upon hearing that the Federals were there, "turned off the road, passed Holman's mills to get [to] Buckingham road and at night put up at Dr. Corborne's near Curdsville." Walter passed through Farmville early on the afternoon of April 6. He reported that the "Yanks were then a few miles from the place." During the day, Joel Garnett and Catlett Taliaferro, both members of Company C, were captured. Garnett was captured at Farmville and sent to Point Lookout, but Catlett, probably captured during the fighting at Sailor's Creek, escaped.[115]

Grant sent a letter to Lee on April 7, to which Lee replied by asking for terms. The fragments of the Army of Northern Virginia continued to move west, but Grant's army was quickly closing in. Walter recorded in his diary that his party set out for Prince Edward Court House. "Met the Yanks when within a mile of C. H. Took the road to Pamplin's Depot. At night stopped with Mr. Rice near Pamplin's Depot." Walter passed through Appomattox Station on April 8. Believing the army would continue on toward Lynchburg, he and an undisclosed number of men continued toward the west.[116]

That evening, Lee went into camp in the woods on the outskirts of Appomattox Court House. The command staff's wagons were somewhere in the wagon train. Lee met with Generals Longstreet, Fitz Lee and John B. Gordon around a campfire. There was a plan to attempt breaking through the Federal cavalry screen the next morning. If no infantry was positioned behind the cavalry, then it might be possible to push even further west. Lee probably only slept three hours that night—if he slept at all. On the morning of April 9, he dressed in a clean uniform with a dress sword. An attack by General John B. Gordon was indecisive, with Gordon sending back word that he needed reinforcements. All that Lee had were Longstreet's men, who were in the rear and holding off two Federal corps. When word arrived that Gordon needed help, and knowing there was none to send, Lee said, "Then there is nothing left me but to go and see General Grant, and I would rather die a thousand deaths."[117]

After conferring with Longstreet and others, Lee and Colonel Charles Marshall, with Sergeant George Tucker carrying a white handkerchief, rode through the Confederate lines of battle, then through the skirmish lines and toward the Federal lines. They soon encountered a Federal officer bearing a letter from Grant. Lee answered the letter, asking for a meeting between the two commanders. A second note was sent, asking for a suspension of hostilities until after they met. Lee continued to wait. Federal skirmishers soon appeared, advancing toward them, and Lee turned his horse away and headed back toward Confederate lines. The original meeting was scheduled to take place at 10:00 a.m., but it took time to find Grant and his staff. With Lee back behind the lines with Longstreet, word arrived from General Meade after 11:00 am that an informal truce was in effect for an hour. Lee rode toward Gordon's position, dismounted in an apple orchard and sent a third note to Grant. At 12:15 p.m., another flag of truce appeared between

An Alfred Waud sketch of Federal soldiers felling the apple tree under which Lee rested at Appomattox. *Library of Congress.*

the lines. The Federal officer and his orderly met with Lee and Marshall, and possibly Walter Taylor, in the apple orchard. There were at least two couriers of the Thirty-Ninth Battalion present: Lewis Ellis (Company A) and Joshua Johns (Company C). Ellis recalled that Lee "was sitting on a seat made by placing the ends of two fence rails in the fork on an apple tree." The Federal officer "dismounted and approached" Lee, "hat in hand. The General rose, when the military salute was exchanged. The officer then handed him a written paper, which he read and then tore up, with his head hanging down as if in deep thought." Grant had agreed to meet with Lee to discuss the terms of surrender. Lee "then called for his horse, and, attended by Col. W.H. Taylor [*sic*] and Special Courier Johns, rode away in the direction of Appomattox Court House."[118]

Marshall rode ahead to find a suitable meeting place, eventually selecting the McLean home in the village of Appomattox Court House. Lee dismounted and, with Marshall and the Federal officer, entered the house while Johns led the horses to the side of the house, removed their bridles and let them graze on the new spring grass. For half an hour, Lee waited. At 1:30 p.m., the clatter of horses could be heard, and Grant arrived with his staff and several other Federal generals. According to one postwar account, upon the arrival of Grant, Jones turned to a Federal officer and asked: "Who is that dirty-looking little man that just arrived?" Grant and Lee met for an hour and a half, working out the details of the surrender of the Army of Northern Virginia.[119]

In the yard, Johns tended the horses, including Traveler, Lee's favorite mount. One of the Federal officers spied Johns. He was a "soldierly looking orderly in a tattered gray uniform, holding three horses," the Federal officer recalled. After the papers were signed, Lee emerged from the McLean house. He paused, slowly putting on his gauntlets. "Then, apparently recalling his thoughts, he glanced deliberately right and left, and not seeing his horse, he called in a hoarse, half-choked voice: 'Orderly! Orderly!'" the Federal officer wrote. "'Here, General, here,' was the quick response." Lee descended the steps "and stood in front of his horse's head while he was being bridled. As the orderly was buckling the throat-latch, the General reached up and drew the forelock out from under the brow-band, parted and smoothed it, and then gently patted the gray charger's forehead." Lee mounted, and as soon as Marshall and Johns were seated on their horses, Lee "drew up his reins, and, with the Colonel riding on his left, and followed by the orderly, moved at a slow walk across the yard toward the gate." Grant came out of the house and down the stairs, and

Joshua Johns rode with Robert E. Lee and Charles Marshall to the McLean home in Appomattox. *Library of Congress.*

the two former adversaries raised their hats in a salute. With that, Lee, Marshall and Johns rode toward the Confederate lines.[120]

Private Catlett Taliaferro (Company C) also recalled seeing Lee meet Grant. Taliaferro claimed many years after the war that he carried one of the messages that Lee wrote to Grant on April 9. He also stated that he was present when Grant and members of his staff

> *rode up within about fifty yards…and dismounted. I remember he had only his fatigue suit on and the only insignia of rank was on his collar. He met General Lee, shook hands with him, and said "General, I am glad to think that bloodshed is at an end." The only word that was said about a sword was when General Grant turned to General Lee and said, "General, I want to apologize for not having my sword on. It was back at my headquarters in the wagon train and it would have detained me an hour or an hour and a half. I want to stop the bloodshed and came without my sword." General Lee told him that it was perfectly satisfactory. Then General Lee*

General Lee leaving Appomattox Court House. *Battles and Leaders.*

remarked to him, "General Grant, in my confusion I overlooked one thing I intended to ask."…[A]ll the cavalry horses in his army were private property and that he would like for his men to have them…General Grant did not hesitate, but said, "Certainly, they need them to make something to eat with." We moved from there to the McLane house, and there that condition was put in about the horses and the terms were signed up. General Grant soon excused himself, being sick and sent some tents and provisions over for General Lee and his staff.[121]

Lee, Marshall and Johns made their way back into Confederate lines. One staff officer recalled seeing Lee "erect and grand-grander than ever—his army broke up into a loving mob and followed him, holding on to his hands, his feet, his coat, the bridle of his horse, and its mane, weeping and sobbing as if their hearts were breaking.…General Lee's head was not bowed, he held it high as usual, but there was a look of sorrow and pain in his face." Another staff officer recalled the officers and men gathering around Lee, who told them: "'Men, we have fought the war together and I have done the best I could for you. You will be paroled and go to your homes until exchanged.' I looked around and the tears were in many eyes and on many cheeks where they had never been brought by fear." Lee returned to the apple orchard.[122]

Someone found Lee's headquarters wagon, and his tent was pitched for the evening. Sergeant William V. Green (Company A) recalled, "After General Lee's return from his interview with General Grant at Appomattox C.H., in silence and in tears his soldiers gathered around him" and hauled down the Second National flag used as Lee's headquarters flag. Once it was lowered, the Stainless Banner "was cut up and divided among the officers and men of Company A." Green wrote that the piece he received was about five inches square. Lee's original headquarters flag, the First National variant made by his wife and daughters, had been retired in the summer of 1863. The flag was packed away with government papers and sent to Charlotte, North Carolina, where it was discovered and secreted away before the papers were turned over to the Federals.[123]

When the ink was dry on the surrender documents, the Thirty-Ninth Battalion Virginia Cavalry surrendered eighty-five men. Captain Samuel Brown was in command of the battalion. Also present were Quartermaster Eli Hamilton and Assistant Surgeon Thomas Marks. Company A, under the command of Lieutenant William N. Green, surrendered thirty-two men; Company B surrendered four privates; Company C, probably led by Lieutenant Andrew Broaddus, surrendered thirty-two men; and Company D, probably under Sergeant Joshua Passano, surrendered fourteen men. Over twenty-seven thousand Confederates were surrendered by Lee at Appomattox. Not everyone accepted the idea of a parole. Passano refused his parole. He was sent to Washington, D.C., where, on May 9, the "Oath [was] administered."[124]

Lee ordered Colonel Marshall to draft his now-famous General Order No. 9 on the morning of April 10. Once the final draft was approved, copies were made so that corps commanders could make copies of it, then read it to their men. One of the clerks of the Thirty-Ninth Battalion probably copied the original, and the duplicates were taken to Lee for his signature. Stanton Allen, a Federal trooper from Massachusetts, recalled a meeting between Lee and General George Meade on the afternoon of April 10. While the generals conversed, "a sergeant of Meade's escort and a sergeant of Lee's headquarters guard entered into such a heated argument that the interference of several officers of both sides was necessary to prevent them from fighting to a finish." Allen failed to provide the names of either of the sergeants.[125]

It is unclear just when the remaining troopers of the Thirty-Ninth Battalion surrendered. It was probably on April 10, with the remaining members of various cavalry regiments still with the Army. They never had a flag to surrender, but many of the other regiments furled their banners and placed them with their stacked rifled muskets. That afternoon, Lee, along with Walter Taylor, Charles Marshall and Giles Cooke, rode toward Richmond. A borrowed Federal ambulance hauled the ill Cooke. The wagon train also included the headquarters wagon and Lee's old ambulance, driven by Anthony Butts (Company B). Other members of the battalion were obviously along with Lee. James Clark (Company C) was one of those soldiers. Another Confederate officer recalled securing an old horse, and "in company with a trooper of Richardson's battalion, whose home was near Manassas Junction, I fell in with the mounted officers attendant upon the ambulance and followed in the wake." The party was stopped. While Lee and his small entourage were allowed to proceed, the others were searched, as the Federals were looking for horses with government marks. Eventually, they continued on their way. Lee, Marshall, Taylor, Butts and maybe one or two other teamsters from the Thirty-Ninth Battalion arrived in Richmond on April 15. The wagons and their drivers then slipped into history.[126]

There were members of the Thirty-Ninth Battalion scattered over two different states. Some, obviously, had been detailed to carry messages for other commanders. A few were probably out looking for new mounts. Throughout Virginia, battalion members came in seeking their paroles and the same terms offered by to Lee by Grant at Appomattox. Thirty-five troopers came in at Winchester, twenty-one in Staunton, fourteen in Fairfax Court House and nine in Richmond. Overall, one hundred and twenty-eight men came in through June 3. On that day, John Beggs and Richard Price, both former members of Company B, were paroled in Verdiersville, while Bryan Enwright, also of Company B, was paroled in Staunton. A handful of battalion members slipped off and made their way to North Carolina, undoubtedly hoping to link up with the Army of Tennessee and continue the fight. However, at the Bennett Place outside Durham on May 1, General Joseph E. Johnston surrendered his army to the Federals. At least five members of the battalion were present, including Adjutant William Walke and Lieutenant Thomas McKaig, Jr. (Company D).[127]

All that remained was to address the issue of soldiers in Federal prisons. Ten members of the battalion were incarcerated at six different prisoner-of-war camps in the North at the time the surrender proceedings were concluded. At Fort Delaware was Franklin Carter (Company B). He was captured in December 1863 in Newtown, Virginia, and first sent to Wheeling, then Camp Chase and, finally, Fort Delaware. He was released on June 19, 1865, after serving eighteen months in captivity—the longest prison term of any member of the battalion. The last man released was John Belcher (Company C). Belcher was captured in Caroline County in May 1864 and sent to Fort Monroe, then Point Lookout and, finally, Elmira in New York. He was released on June 23.[128]

Those who surrendered with Lee at Appomattox or under Johnston in North Carolina, those paroled later and those who were released from prisoner camps after taking the oath of allegiance began their trek back home to rebuild their lives. Twenty-three men from the Thirty-Ninth Battalion died during the war; disease, whether it was acquired in a Confederate hospital or a Northern POW camp, claimed the majority.

In Retrospect

Lee's Body Guard, or the Thirty-Ninth Battalion Virginia Cavalry, was created in a time of need. Robert E. Lee needed an effective courier service as well as men to act as guides and scouts. In 1861 and 1862, entire companies were taken from cavalry regiments to serve in these roles, diminishing the effectiveness of the mounted arm of the Confederate army. The creation of these four companies (and possibly a fifth) filled that void. The courier battalion was not part of the general or personal staff of Robert E. Lee. It was a separate organization or command. However, it was an integral part of that military family. The members of that battalion were the clerks who copied orders and messengers who delivered telegrams from the telegraph office, and during battle, they were the riders who looked for stragglers and escorted prisoners to Richmond. During the war, they were often under fire, especially while carrying messages to commanders.

J. Boone Bartholomees Jr., in his seminal work, *Buff Facings and Gilt Buttons: Staff and Headquarters Operations in the Army of Northern Virginia*, considers the couriers, orderlies and escorts "almost historically invisible." That is very true. In numerous books written by Confederate staff officers, couriers are seldom mentioned; even when they are mentioned, the officer seldom calls the courier by name. In September 1862, around the time the Thirty-Ninth Battalion was being formed, Henry Kyd Douglas recalled seeing Stonewall Jackson sending a message to Lee that Harpers Ferry had fallen. "By the same courier, I sent a card to my father," Douglas wrote, but the courier remains anonymous. Campbell Brown, serving on the staff of Richard Ewell, wrote that during the Gettysburg campaign, he bore a message to Lee. Brown set out with two couriers. One was sent back to Ewell not long after the trio departed, and the other left with Lee "to follow the next morning." Once again, the names of the two couriers have been lost to history.[129]

"The 39th Virginia Cavalry Battalion was an army asset," Bartholomees wrote. While the companies bore names like "Lee's Body Guard" and "Ewell's Body Guard," connecting specific men to individual generals is difficult. Ideally, one company would have worked with Lee, while the other three, after June 1863, were assigned to the other three corps. It seems like most of the men in Ewell's Body Guard (Company B) were assigned to Richard Ewell, then to Stonewall Jackson. However, it is noted in William Allmand's (Company B) compiled service record that he was assigned to Jackson. Company C was known as Lee's Body Guard. However, one Company C member, Catlett Taliaferro, stated that he belonged to Jackson's staff. Other Company C members were attached to other generals: George Kennedy worked for General Early, while William H. Jenkins was riding with A.P. Hill the morning he was killed. Franklin Walter (Company A) often wrote in his diary that he was with Lee at various times during the war. Thomas Upshur (Company B) stated he was a member of "Ewell's escort and after he was wounded with Gen. Early until Fredericksburg. Transferred Stonewall Jackson's Headquarters…for Second Corps until after Gettysburg. On returning to Va., was assigned to…Lee's Headquarters." In all likelihood, details were sent out from the battalion to generals on an as-needed basis.[130]

While the cavalry companies that had been used as couriers were sent back to their respective regiments beginning in late 1862, other non-battalion men were employed in a courier role. Often called the chief of couriers for A.P. Hill's corps, Sergeant George W. Tucker was not a member of the Thirty-Ninth Battalion. Moxley Sorrel, on Longstreet's staff, recalled that during the Overland Campaign, "perhaps two dozen" officers and couriers were taking shelter from artillery "under the lee of a gable" of a house. "We knew it would not resist a shell, but could fend off the offensive fragments." A shell soon struck one of the chimneys, raining bricks on those below. Sorrel noted that two of the couriers, whom he identified as Hardy and Tucker, were wounded. There actually were no Hardys in the battalion, although there were two men with the last name Tucker; neither was reported wounded. In the postwar writings of Henry Kyd Douglas, Jed Hotchkiss, Campbell Brown and others, there are scores of other examples that illustrate the anonymity of the couriers or cases of mistaken identity.[131]

Being a courier was fraught with danger regardless of one's identity. Twenty-one members of the battalion died during the war. Two members perished from wounds received in battle. Five died of disease while they were prisoners of war. The other fourteen died of disease, mostly in hospitals around central Virginia. Seventeen other battalion members were wounded in action. Forty-eight battalion members were captured and incarcerated during the war. Several took the oath of allegiance and were released north of Virginia. Only one, Charles Caldwell (Company B), joined the Union army after taking the oath.

Then, there is the case of the fifth company. In the records of the Library of Virginia is a folder marked "Captain John W. Opie's Co." There are a mere five names listed in this company: John W. Opie, captain; P.M. Dice; J.A. Henkle; B.G. Turk; and John W. Wallace. It is unclear precisely who John W. Opie was. There was a John N. Opie who served in the Sixth Virginia Cavalry, at times riding with Mosby's command. However, in John N. Opie's postwar book, he never makes mention of attempting to raise a company of scouts, guides and couriers.[132]

For a group of men who spent a considerable time with the ranking generals of the Army of Northern Virginia, very few members of the Thirty-Ninth Virginia left accounts of their wartime experiences. Captain William Randolph wrote about Chancellorsville, and Catlett Taliaferro wrote of the Wilderness and Spotsylvania Court House, but his accounts are sometimes unverifiable. Occasionally, the old veterans wrote to local newspapers about some specific event. In 1892, John Rodes wrote about being one of Lee's couriers at Gettysburg. A year before, William Page wrote about meeting General Lee early in 1861 and talking with the general again at Appomattox. Lewis Ellis (Company A) likewise wrote about Appomattox and seeing Lee in the apple orchard while awaiting word from Grant. James Denney wrote of delivering notes to Longstreet during the Gettysburg campaign.[133]

After the war, most of the veterans simply returned to their homes and families to pick up the pieces of their lives. William Randolph, who raised the very first company, was reported captured after Gettysburg and was held as a prisoner of war at Johnson's Island until the war ended. He lived in Mississippi for a number of years but eventually returned to Fauquier County, where he passed away on July 31, 1914. "Stonewall Jackson's Aide Dead" was the newspaper headline announcing Randolph's demise. His death announcement made national news and appeared in newspapers from New York to Cincinnati.[134]

William F. Randolph is buried in Warrenton, Virginia. *Michael C. Hardy.*

Augustus Pifer organized the second company of the battalion. In mid-March 1865, Pifer was relieved of command for unknown reasons. He went on to study law, and around 1868, he moved to Newberry, South Carolina, where he became the principal of Newberry Academy. Pifer was active in the United Confederate Veterans and the Masonic Lodge. When he passed away in Newberry in 1907, local newspapers made mention of his role as "captain of General Robert E. Lee's body guard and his comrades in arms say that in those days when courage was put to test at the point of steel and at the mouth of the cannon, he did his duty."[135]

Major John H. Richardson returned to Richmond after the war. Richardson was with the battalion through February 1865, and a postwar newspaper article claimed he was with the battalion at Appomattox, but he does not appear on any of the parole records. Back in Richmond, he served thirteen years as the city's gas inspector and, later, as deputy clerk of the chancery court. He also operated a streetcar line. Richardson was considered "one of Richmond's best-known citizens, a man who was devoted to Virginia, her traditions and her people." He passed away in Richmond on November 29, 1900.[136]

Commanding the battalion at Appomattox was Captain Samuel Brown. He returned to Augusta County and farmed there until he headed to Fort Valley, Georgia, where he died in May 1903. William Page, who organized what became Company D, also survived the war. A student at Hampden-Sydney College as the war began, Page was last reported as with the battalion toward the end of 1864. He was granted a furlough in November–December 1864 and does not appear again in official records. However, Page wrote after the war that he talked with Lee at Appomattox. Page went on to earn a doctor of divinity degree from Princeton Theological Seminary and worked with Presbyterian and Episcopal churches in New York City before becoming rector of St. Paul's Church in Cornwell, New York. He was active in veterans' affairs. The idea for what became the New York Division of the United Confederate Veterans was born in his study at the rectory of his church in New York City in February 1890. Page helped draft the constitution, then served as chaplain, regularly attending the annual Robert E. Lee birthday banquet at the New York Hotel. Captain Page died in 1920 and was hailed as the "Last of Lee's Staff," although he was officially a member of the Thirty-Ninth Battalion.[137]

The rank and file also worked to rebuild their lives. Isaac Hite headed to Cooper County, Missouri, where he married, raised a family and farmed. Franklin Walter stayed in Virginia, living to the ripe old age of ninety-four before he passed away in 1930. Walter owned a store, dealt in wool and worked at a bank. A. Carter Atkinson held public office, first as Virginia's Commonwealth attorney, then in the Virginia legislature and, finally, as the mayor of Manchester. Marshall Brown moved to West Virginia and became a conductor on the Baltimore & Ohio Railroad. James Denny settled in Baltimore, Maryland, and became involved in politics. Denny served on the Baltimore City Council, in the Maryland House of Delegates, on the Baltimore School Board and for two terms (1899–1901 and 1903–1905) in the U.S. House of Representatives.[138]

Captain W.W. Page survived the war, earned a divinity degree, then moved to New York. *The National Magazine.*

Many of these men were proud of their service as couriers for General Lee, and their obituaries made mention of that pride. Albert Miller was "Lee's courier for four years." A headline in Washington, D.C., announcing the death of Samuel Franklin in 1921 read: "Gen. R.E. Lee's Courier is Dead." Another 1921 obituary, this one for John Burkholder, proudly proclaimed he was a "member of General Lee's Bodyguard." James Kinnier's obituary in 1904 stated the same—he was a member of "Lee's Bodyguard." The service of members of the battalion even trickled into the obituaries of their widows. Isabella Woods passed away in 1926. Her obituary mentioned her work in church, that she came from a prominent family and that her husband "was one of General Robert E. Lee's couriers during the war between the states." However, the obituary never mentions the name of her husband, Thomas Woods, who had passed away in 1911.[139]

John W. Towson claimed service in the Thirty-Ninth Battalion many years after the war. *Confederate Veteran.*

Many of the old soldiers earnestly sought to put the war behind them. James Carico headed west after the war, settling in Kansas. In 1885, he presented a large silk Federal flag to his local Grand Army of the Republic post. A local newspaper reported Carico's sentiment on the occasion. Carico "said he held the old soldiers of the union in high esteem, and knew of no better way of expressing his feeling for them and the old flag, than by giving to their keeping a banner that in its newness should indicate the higher glory of the union and the revival of a united brotherhood."[140]

John Hall passed away in Prince William County, Virginia, in 1931. His obituary is a fitting conclusion to the story of the Thirty-Ninth Battalion Virginia Cavalry. Hall had served as a "bodyguard and courier for General Robert. E. Lee." Hall had been captured at Gettysburg and imprisoned, released and "honorably discharged at Winchester." He had spent time with Jackson, Lee and a host of others. At the end of his funeral service, after a sermon and the singing of his favorite hymns, the United Daughters of the Confederacy provided a flag; then, the "Stars and Bars, for which he had fought so bravely, and had cherished so dearly throughout his long life, were lovingly enfolded about his earthly remains and laid to rest with him."[141]

THIRTY-NINTH BATTALION VIRGINIA ROSTER

T he roster for the Thirty-Ninth Battalion is taken from the Compiled Military Service Records, M324, Rolls 197–199, Record Group 199, National Archives; the roster in Robert Driver and Kevin Ruffner's *1st Battalion Virginia Infantry, 39th Battalion Virginia Cavalry, 24th Battalion Virginia Partisan Rangers*; and searches in newspapers and on the Find a Grave and Ancestry websites. While every measure has been taken to ensure accuracy, there undoubtedly are discrepancies. Names marked with an asterisk (*) are not in the compiled service records; their names appear on postwar rosters or pension applications. AWOL = a soldier who was absent without leave. NFR = "No Further Record." Unless otherwise specified, all place names refer to locations in Virginia.

Adams, James T. Private, Company C. Born 1830. Enlisted Lynchburg November 10, 1862. Present through December 1864. Died 1896.

Allen, Charles. Private, Company D. Born circa 1836. Place and date of enlistment unknown. Paroled Fairfax Court House May 1, 1865.

Allen, John C. Private, Company D. Enlisted Richmond February 12, 1864. Paroled Richmond April 21, 1865.

Allen, Thompson C. Private, Company D. Enlisted Danville June 10, 1863. Transferred to Thirty-Eighth Virginia Infantry November 17, 1864, in exchange for T.M. Carter. Died 1890. Interred Green Hill Cemetery, Danville.

Allmand, William D. Third Sergeant, Company B. Enlisted Richmond August 12, 1862. Mustered in as fourth sergeant; promoted to third sergeant on unknown date. Absent recruiting horses March–April 1863. Reported captured at Gettysburg, July 1–3, 1863; however, this is not substantiated by Federal records. Paroled Richmond April 12, 1865.

Antrim, William W. Private, Company C. Born 1845. Enlisted at Orange Court House August 6, 1863. Court-martialed and fined one month's pay August 10, 1864. Paroled Appomattox Court House April 9, 1865. Died 1886. Interred Maplewood Cemetery, Charlottesville.

Armistead, James A. Sergeant Major, Field and Staff. Born 1841. Previously served as drill instructor and on staff of Brigadier General Montgomery Corse. Enlisted Lynchburg September 1, 1862. Mustered in as a private, Company C. Promoted to sergeant major and transferred to Field and Staff on unknown date. Wounded in action at Chancellorsville, May 2–3, 1863. Wounded in action at Gettysburg July 2, 1863. Paroled Lynchburg May 26, 1865. Died 1907. Interred Oak Hill Cemetery, Polk County, Florida.

Arnold, John W. Private, Company A. Born 1843. Previously served in Fifth Virginia Infantry. Transferred October 11, 1862. Captured Warrenton December 20, 1862, and paroled. Returned to company December 31, 1862. Reported absent sick August 31, 1863. Paroled Winchester April 19, 1865. Died 1915. Interred Queen's Point Cemetery, Kayser, West Virginia.

Atkinson, A. Carter. ---. Born 1848. Place and date of enlistment unknown. Paroled Richmond April 28, 1865. Died 1902. Interred Hollywood Cemetery, Richmond.

Atkinson, H. Private, Company B. Place and date of enlistment unknown. Paroled Richmond April 19, 1865.

Avery, William. Private, Company D. Enlisted in Greenwich July 6, 1863. NFR.

Ayres, James. Private, Company B. Born 1833. Enlisted Orange Court House August 18, 1862. Deserted near Millwood November 1, 1862. NFR. Died 1917. Interred St. George's Episcopal Church Cemetery, Accomack County.

*Baber, John. Private, Company E. Born 1845. Died 1931. Interred Hillsborough Baptist Church Cemetery, Albemarle County.

Baber, Richard S. Private, Company C. Born circa 1835. Previously served in Forty-Sixth Virginia Infantry. Enlisted Lynchburg September 23, 1862. Present or accounted for until December 1864. NFR. Interred Neriah Baptist Church Cemetery, Rockbridge County.

Bagby, Lilborne C. Private, Company C. Born circa 1831. Previously served in Second Virginia Cavalry. Enlisted Lynchburg January 10, 1863. Present until furloughed August 1863. Absent sick April 12, 1864. Paroled Lynchburg April 14, 1865. Died 1875.

*Baker, Alexander. Captain, Quartermaster, Field and Staff. Born 1814. Place and date of enlistment unknown. Promoted and transferred to unknown regiment. Died 1892. Interred Old Chapel Cemetery, Clarke County.

Baker, Jacob E. Private, Company A. Born 1828. Enlisted Orange Court House August 16, 1863. Present or accounted for until captured near Germantown, North Carolina, April 10, 1865. Sent to Nashville. Transferred to Louisville, then Camp Chase, Ohio. Took oath of allegiance and was released June 13, 1865. Died 1906. Interred Mount Hebron Cemetery, Winchester.

Baker, James M. Private, Company A. Enlisted Orange Court House January 7, 1864. Absent sick October 28–31, 1864. Absent on horse detail December 24–31, 1864. Paroled at Louisa Court House May 15, 1865. Died 1918. Interred St. John's Lutheran Church Cemetery, Frederick County.

Baker, John R. Private, Company A, Born 1846. Enlisted Winchester October 11, 1862. Present until reported absent without leave May 10, 1864. Transferred to Sixth Virginia Cavalry March 1, 1865. Died 1901. Interred Stonewall Cemetery, Winchester.

*Baker, Martin R. Private, Company A. Born 1820. Place and date of enlistment unknown. Died 1901. Interred Mount Hebron Cemetery, Winchester.

Baker, William M. Private, Company A. Born 1835. Enlisted Winchester October 11, 1862. Absent November 18, 1862, until transferred to Sixth Virginia Cavalry. Died 1914. Interred Greenhill Cemetery, Stephens City.

Ballard, William G. Private, Company C. Born circa 1840. Previously served in Fifty-Sixth Virginia Infantry. Enlisted Staunton February 1, 1863. Absent without leave February 28–August 31, 1863. "Believed to have joined infantry company." NFR.

Balthorpe, George R. Second Lieutenant, Company A. Born 1839. Elected third lieutenant October 11, 1862. Present or accounted for until resignation on September 8, 1864. Reenlisted in Forty-Third Battalion Virginia Cavalry. Died 1918. Interred Linville Cemetery, Knox County, Missouri.

Bandy, Calvin J. Private, Company C. Born 1845. Enlisted Orange Court House February 14, 1864. Present or accounted for through 1864. Paroled at Appomattox Court House April 9, 1865. Died 1866. Interred Crockett-Bandy Cemetery, Roanoke County.

Baxter, William F. Private, Company B. Enlisted Winchester October 2, 1862. Transferred to Thirty-Fifth Battalion Virginia Cavalry April 22, 1863.

Beaver, Daniel. Private, Company B. Born 1820. Enlisted Orange Court House September 1, 1863. Reported present October–December 1864. NFR. Died 1901. Interred Beaver Cemetery, Shenandoah County.

Beggs, John. Private, Company B. Enlisted Orange Court House August 18, 1862. Reported present November 1862–October 1863, March 1864. Issued clothing March 1864. Paroled near Verdiersville June 4, 1865.

Belcher, John J. Private, Company D. Enlisted Danville May 1, 1863. Captured Caroline County May 9, 1864. Sent to Fort Monroe and transferred to Elmira, New York. Took the oath and was released June 23, 1865.

Bell, James H. Private, Company C. Born circa 1839. Previously served in Seventh Virginia Cavalry. Enlisted Orange Court House February 16, 1864. Reported AWOL November 5, 1864. Paroled Gordonsville May 20, 1865.

Bethell, William B. Private, Company B. Born 1844. Place and date of enlistment unknown. Present in 1865. Died 1915. Interred Green Hill Cemetery, Danville.

Bishop, Edward F. Private, Company C. Born 1842. Enlisted Lynchburg January 8, 1863. Reported sick in a Charlottesville hospital, "debilitas," August 3–31, 1863. Court-martialed December 26, 1862. Discharged by reason of disease of the heart June 12, 1864. Died 1913. Interred Hammond Chapel Cemetery, Augusta County.

Black, Charles O. Private, Company A. Born 1835. Enlisted Winchester October 11, 1862. Present or accounted for through April 1863. Listed as company teamster May 9–August 31, 1863. Absent on horse detail October 10–31, 1864. Paroled Appomattox Court House April 9, 1865. Died 1910. Interred Keezletown Cemetery, Rockingham County.

Booker, John R. Private, Company D. Born 1840. Previously served in Twentieth Virginia Infantry. Enlisted Richmond February 19, 1863. Absent sick with "gonorrhoea" in a Danville hospital July 20–August 1, 1863. Present November 11, 1863. NFR. Died 1902. Interred Hollywood Cemetery, Richmond.

*Booker, Wesley. Private, Company A.

Boswell, James C. Private, Company C. Enlisted Orange Court House January 20, 1864. Captured Cold Harbor, June 1, 1864. Sent to Point Lookout and transferred to Elmira, New York, where he died of typhoid fever September 23, 1864. Interred Woodlawn Cemetery, Elmira, New York.

Bowe, Henry C. Private, Company D. Previously served in Thirty-Eighth Virginia Infantry. Enlisted Danville August 15, 1863, without permission. Returned to Thirty-Eighth Virginia.

Bowen, Marion A. Private, Company C. Born 1826. Enlisted Lynchburg January 1, 1863. Present or accounted for through August 8, 1863 and August–December 1864. NFR. Died 1914. Interred Mount Moriah Methodist Church Cemetery, Albemarle County.

Bowles, Drury W. Private, Company D. Born 1847. Enlisted Petersburg November 13, 1864. Present through December 31, 1864. Paroled Appomattox Court House April 9, 1865. Died 1919. Interred Hollywood Cemetery, Richmond.

Bowles, James H. Private, Company D. Enlisted Orange Court House March 24, 1864. Reported in a Petersburg hospital June 17, 1864. Wounded in action in left hand and admitted to a Richmond hospital June 20, 1864. Furloughed June 23, 1864, for forty days. Later reported on duty with General Hoke. Paroled at Appomattox Court House April 9, 1865. Interred Bowles Cemetery, Goochland County.

Bradner, James A. Private, Company D. Enlisted Danville May 25, 1863. Present or accounted for through September 1, 1863. Captured Caroline County, May 9, 1863. Sent to Fort Monroe; transferred to Point Lookout, Maryland; then Elmira, New York. Died October 9, 1864, of chronic diarrhea. Interred Woodlawn Cemetery, Elmira, New York.

Brill, Henry L. Private, Company A. Born 1830. Enlisted Winchester October 11, 1862. Absent sick November 19, 1862–August 31, 1863. Reported AWOL September 29–December 31, 1864. Paroled Winchester April 22, 1865. Died 1896. Interred Gravel Springs Cemetery, Frederick County.

*Brill, Samuel. Private, Company A. Born 1824. Previously served in Eleventh Virginia Cavalry. NFR. Died 1908. Interred Gravel Hill Cemetery, Frederick County.

Britton, John N. Private, Company C. Born 1846. Enlisted Petersburg October 1864. Absent on leave March 1865. Paroled Staunton May 20, 1865. Died 1932. Interred New Providence Presbyterian Church Cemetery, Rockbridge County.

Broaddus, Andrew J. Third Lieutenant, Company C. Born 1840. Mustered in as private at Luray December 20, 1862. Elected third lieutenant

March 9, 1863. Horse killed in Berkley County September 1863. Court-martialed for conduct unbecoming an officer December 7, 1863. Present through September 1863. AWOL December 12–31,1864. Paroled at Appomattox Court House April 9, 1865. Died 1898. Interred Green Hill Cemetery, Page County.

*Brooke, C.W. Private, company unknown. Place and date of enlistment unknown. Furloughed September 1, 1864. NFR.

Brooks, James U. Private, Company D. Enlisted Orange Court House March 24, 1864. NFR.

*Brown, Adam W. Private, Company A. Born 1839. Died 1910. Interred Centenary Reformed UCC Cemetery, Winchester.

Brown, John W. Private, Company A. Born 1847. Enlisted Winchester October 11, 1862. Present September–December 1864. NFR. Died 1908. Interred Rhodesville Baptist Church Cemetery, Orange County.

Brown, Marshall H. Private, Company C. Born 1845. Previously served in Tenth Virginia Infantry and Captain Avis's Provost Guard. Transferred to Thirty-Ninth Battalion January 28, 1863. Present or accounted for until paroled Staunton on May 17, 1865. Died 1918. Interred Bluemont Cemetery, Taylor County, West Virginia.

Brown, Samuel B., Jr. Captain, Company C. Born 1841. Previously served in Fifty-Second Virginia Infantry. Elected captain, Thirty-Ninth Battalion March 9, 1863. Present until reported sick September–October 1864. Returned to duty November–December 1864. Reported commanding battalion at Appomattox Court House and paroled April 9, 1865. Died 1903. Interred Oaklawn Cemetery, Fort Valley, Georgia.

Brown, William. Private, Company B. Born 1848. Enlisted Staunton January 7, 1863. Detailed as teamster December 1863–December 1864. Paroled at Appomattox April 9, 1864.

Broy, Elijah N. Private, Company A. Born 1809. Enlisted Winchester October 11, 1862. Reported AWOL November 28, 1862–September 16, 1863. Arrested and sent to Richmond. Reported in a Richmond hospital with debility October 11–November 22, 1863. Court-martialed for desertion January 27, 1864. Detailed provost guard, Staunton. NFR. Died 1874.

*Brubaker, C.W. Private, Company B. Born 1841. Died 1920. Interred Green Hill Cemetery, Clarke County.

*Bruen, M.A. Private, Company B or C. Died 1900.

Brumback, Joseph C. Private, Company B. Born 1841. Previously served in Dixie Artillery and Cayce's Virginia Artillery. Transferred to battalion January 21, 1863. Present or accounted for through December 1864. NFR. Died 1932. Interred Green Hill Cemetery, Page County.

Bucher, James R.S. Private, Company A. Born 1932. Previously served in Fifty-First Virginia Militia. Enlisted in battalion in Fredericksburg May 1, 1863. Present or accounted for through December 1864. Paroled Winchester April 22, 1865. Died 1916. Interred St. John's Lutheran Church Cemetery, Frederick County.

Burch, G.C. Corporal, Company B. Enlisted Richmond October 29, 1862. Present through October 31, 1863. Transferred to Maryland Line March 31, 1864. NFR.

Burk, Francis. Private, Company B. Enlisted Richmond February 18, 1863. Present until reported AWOL March 1864. NFR.

*Burkholder, John W. Private, Company C. Born 1842. Died 1921. Interred Greenville Methodist Church Cemetery, Augusta County.

Butt, James W. Private, Company A. Born 1846. Enlisted Winchester October 11, 1862. Present through April 1863. Transferred to Twelfth Virginia Cavalry.

Butts, Anthony S. Private, Company B. Born 1840. Enlisted Culpeper Court House August 1, 1863. Detailed as teamster in quartermaster's department, August 7, 1864–December 31, 1864. Paroled at Appomattox April 9, 1865. Died 1891. Interred St. Mary's Catholic Cemetery, Norfolk.

Caldwell, Charles B. Private, Company C. Enlisted Orange Court House August 18, 1862. Present or accounted for until captured July 3, 1863, at Gettysburg, Pennsylvania. Sent to Fort Delaware, Delaware. Took oath and joined Third Maryland Cavalry (U.S.) September 22, 1863.

Camden, John A. Private, Company A. Enlisted Orange Court House August 18, 1862. Present or accounted for as bugler November 1862–April 1863. Captured in Pennsylvania July 5, 1863. Sent to hospital in Frederick, Maryland, with "debilitas." Transferred to Annapolis, Maryland. Paroled and released on unknown date and rejoined battalion prior to December 8, 1864. NFR.

Camden, William. Private, Company B. Place and date of enlistment unknown. Reported AWOL October 1862. NFR.

Campbell, Bean C. Private, Company A. Born 1840. Enlisted Winchester October 11, 1862. Reported absent sick in Richmond November 27, 1863, with "billious fever." Furloughed January 3, 1864 for thirty days. Present September–November 1864. Reported AWOL December 17–31, 1864. Paroled Winchester April 17, 1865. Died 1918. Interred Mount Hebron Cemetery, Winchester.

Campbell, Robert M. Private, Company A. Born 1844. Enlisted Culpeper Court House July 24, 1863. Reported present or accounted for on surviving muster roll sheets. Paroled Winchester April 18, 1865. Died 1930. Interred Cheatham Cemetery, Wilson County, Kansas.

Campbell, Thomas. Private, Company A. Enlisted Winchester October 11, 1862. Deserted November 19, 1862.

Campbell, William. Private, Company B. Enlisted Bunker Hill October 4, 1862. Deserted near Millwood November 1, 1862.

Cannon, John G. Private, Company B. Enlisted Orange Court House August 18, 1862. Reported AWOL October 20–December 31, 1862. In a Richmond hospital April 11, 1863. Captured at an undisclosed location and on unknown date in 1863. Paroled and transferred to the First Maryland Cavalry April 21, 1864.

Carpenter, William H. Private, Company B. Enlisted Richmond October 29, 1862. Absent recruiting horses March–April 1863. Captured Gettysburg, Pennsylvania, July 4, 1863. Sent to Fort Delaware. Died of disease September 15, 1863. Interred Finn's Point, New Jersey.

Carr, Edward F. Private, Company B. Born 1839. Enlisted Orange Court House August 18, 1862. Absent recruiting horses April 20–30, 1863. Reported present or accounted for on surviving muster roll sheets until paroled Fairfax Court House May 28, 1865.

Carrico, James M. Private, Company C. Born 1844. Previously served in Twenty-Fourth Virginia Infantry. Enlisted Lynchburg November 20, 1862. Reported present or accounted for on surviving muster roll sheets until August 1863. NFR.

Carrico, William F. Private, Company A. Born 1841. Enlisted Winchester October 11, 1862. Absent sick with typhoid fever in a Charlottesville hospital August 23–September 17, 1863. Absent with fractured forearm in a Charlottesville hospital January 1–February 13, 1864. Absent on horse detail December 24–31, 1864. Paroled at Appomattox Court House April 9, 1865. Died 1913. Interred Carrico Family Cemetery, Prince William County.

Carter, Charles W. Private, Company B. Born 1846. Enlisted Haymarket September 30, 1862. Absent recruiting horses May 5–6, 1863. Reported AWOL September 15–October 31, 1863. NFR. Died 1929. Interred Maplewood Cemetery, Charlottesville.

Carter, Christopher L. Private, Company D. Previously served in Thirty-Eighth Virginia Infantry. Transferred to battalion December 6, 1864 in exchange for George W. King. On horse detail December 31, 1864. NFR.

Carter, Franklin B. Private, Company A. Born 1832. Enlisted Winchester October 11, 1862. Captured Newton December 29, 1863, and sent to Wheeling, West Virginia. Transferred to Camp Chase, Ohio, then Fort Delaware. Paroled and released June 19, 1865. Died 1895. Interred Stones Chapel Cemetery, Clarke County.

Carter, John H. Private, Company B. Born 1840. Enlisted Orange Court House August 18, 1862. Captured Loudoun County prior to October 31, 1863. NFR. Died 1909. Interred Marshall Cemetery, Fauquier County.

Carter, Lawrence P. Private, Company A. Born 1842. Previously served in Thirteenth Virginia Infantry. Enlisted Winchester October 11, 1862. Reported present or accounted for on surviving muster roll sheets. Paroled at Appomattox April 9, 1865.

Carter, Thomas M. Quartermaster Sergeant, Field and Staff. Previously served in Thirty-Eighth Virginia Infantry. Transferred to battalion November 1864 in exchange for Thompson C. Allen. Mustered in as a private, Company D. Promoted to quartermaster sergeant December 31, 1864, and transferred to Field and Staff. Paroled April 25, 1865.

Cartmell, Robert M. Third Lieutenant, Company A. Born 1834. Enlisted Winchester October 11, 1862. Mustered in as first sergeant. Elected third lieutenant November 14, 1864. Paroled Winchester April 24, 1865. Died 1902. Interred Old Cartmell Cemetery, Frederick County.

Casey, William. Private, Company B. Enlisted Bunker Hill October 17, 1862. Absent recruiting horses March–April 1863. Issued clothing March 1864. NFR.

Catterton, Benjamin H. Private, Company B. Born 1846. Enlisted September 1863 but location unknown. Paroled Charlottesville May 17, 1865. Died 1919. Interred Greenwood Cemetery, Gregg County, Texas.

Catterton, William W. Private, Company C. Born 1845. Enlisted Lynchburg December 1, 1862. Reported present or accounted for on surviving muster roll sheets. Paroled at Appomattox April 9, 1865. Died 1924. Interred Catterton Cemetery, Orange County.

Chamblin, George. Private, Company A. Enlisted Winchester October 11, 1862. Deserted November 1, 1862. Also served in Thirty-Fifth Battalion Virginia Cavalry.

Childress, David D. Private, Company C. Born 1842. Previously served in Twenty-Fifth Virginia Infantry. Enlisted in battalion in Staunton December 16, 1862. Returned to Twenty-Fifth Virginia January–April 1864. Died 1925. Interred Riverview Cemetery, Augusta County.

Childress, R.H. Private, Company D. Born 1843. Enlisted Camp Lee February 18, 1863. NFR.

Childress, William. Private, Company C. Born 1845. Previously served in Twenty-Fifth Virginia Infantry. Enlisted Staunton December 16, 1862. Captured June 15, 1864 at unknown place. Exchanged on unknown date. Paroled Staunton May 15, 1865.

Christian, Nathaniel H. Sergeant, Company C. Born 1843. Previous drillmaster Second North Carolina. Enlisted Lynchburg September 15, 1862. Mustered in as a private. Promoted to sergeant prior to October 1, 1864. Absent sick December 13–31, 1864. Paroled at Appomattox April 9, 1865. Died 1913. Interred Old Catholic Cemetery, Galveston County, Texas.

*Chumbley, Joseph H. Private, Company E. Born 1844. Died 1917. Interred Hickman Cemetery, Pulaski County.

Chumby, James H. Private, Company C. Enlisted Lynchburg November 7, 1862. Absent sick with pneumonia in a Richmond hospital April 15, 1864. Absent sick with "erthema" in a Richmond Hospital July 16, 1864. Present until December 1864. NFR.

Claiter, William. Private, Company C. Enlisted Richmond February 18, 1863. Reported present or accounted through February 28, 1863. AWOL March 1863. NFR.

Clark, James W. Private, Company C. Born 1831. Enlisted Orange Court House March 16, 1864. Reported present or accounted for on surviving muster roll sheets. Paroled Appomattox Court House April 9, 1865. Died 1917. Interred East Mount Cemetery, Greenville, Texas.

Clement, William T. Corporal, Company D. Born 1828. Previously served Eleventh Virginia Infantry. Transferred to Thirty-Ninth Battalion

September 13, 1863. Mustered in as a corporal. Paroled Columbia May 2, 1865. Died 1888. Interred Champion Cemetery, Fluvanna County.

Clyne, William C. Private, Company B. Enlisted Orange Court House August 18, 1862. Reported present or accounted for through October 31, 1863. NFR.

Cockerille, Phillip W. Private, Company A. Enlisted Culpeper Court House July 31, 1863. Present through August 31, 1863. Absent sick with pneumonia in a Richmond hospital April 13, 1864. Died April 20, 1864.

Codwise, Beverly R. Sergeant, Company C. Born 1841. Previously served in Twenty-Fifth Virginia Infantry. Enlisted Thirty-Ninth Battalion July 1, 1863, Gettysburg, Pennsylvania. Promoted to sergeant prior to January 1864. Captured Martinsburg July 9, 1864. Sent to Wheeling, West Virginia. Transferred to Camp Chase. Took oath and released December 16, 1864. Died 1924. Interred Rockville Cemetery, Montgomery County, Maryland.

Coiner, George M. Private, Company C. Born 1841. Previously served in Fifty-Second Virginia. Enlisted Thirty-Ninth Battalion Orange Court House January 20, 1864. Presented September–December 1864. Paroled Staunton May 17, 1865. Died 1912. Interred Trinity Lutheran Church Cemetery, Augusta County.

Coleman, Thomas. Private, Company B. Place and date of enlistment unknown. AWOL. October 1862. NFR.

*Colter, ---. Private, Company B. Place and date of enlistment unknown. NFR.

Comer, James M. Private, Company D. Born 1832. Previously served in Sixth Virginia Cavalry and Thirty-Eighth Virginia Infantry. Transferred to Thirty-Ninth Battalion September 30, 1864. Reported present or accounted for on surviving muster roll sheets. NFR. Died 1897. Interred Comer-Harvey Cemetery, Pittsylvania County.

Compton, James B. Private, Company C. Born 1843. Enlisted Luray February 8, 1863. Reported AWOL through April 1863. Transferred to Forty-Ninth Virginia Infantry on unknown date. Died 1927. Interred Green Hill Cemetery, Page County.

Connaway, Martin. Private, Company A. Place and date of enlistment unknown. Reported AWOL October 1862. NFR.

Conrad, B.F. Private, Company A. Born 1842. Place and date of enlistment unknown. Wounded in action on unknown date and admitted to the Gordonsville hospital June 15, 1864; transferred to a Charlottesville hospital that same day. NFR. Died 1882. Interred Upperville Methodist Church Cemetery, Fauquier County.

Cooper, Jackson Amos. Private, Company A. Born 1845. Enlisted Berryville June 22, 1863. Reported as battalion teamster September–December 1864. Paroled at Appomattox Court House April 9, 1865. Died 1928. Interred Hollywood Cemetery, Richmond.

Cooper, Henry J. Private, Company A. Born 1835. Enlisted Winchester October 11, 1862. Reported present or accounted for on surviving muster roll sheets. Paroled Winchester April 22, 1865. Died 1908. Interred Lutheran Cemetery, Hampshire County, West Virginia.

*Cooper, Jackson A. Private, Company A.

Cooper, Watson C. Private, Company A. Born 1837. Enlisted Winchester October 11, 1862. Detailed as saddler November 1862–December 1864. Paroled at Winchester April 22, 1865. Died 1897. Interred Gravel Springs Cemetery, Frederick County.

Corbin, Ralph J. Private, Company B. Born 1834. Enlisted Richmond October 29, 1862. Absent sick with bronchitis in a Richmond hospital February 10, 1863. Died June 2, 1863. Interred Corbin Cemetery, Accomack County.

Corner, James M. Private, Company D. Previously served in Thirtieth Virginia Infantry. Enlisted Danville September 20, 1864. Present through December 31, 1864. NFR.

Cotter, John. Private, Company B. Born 1841. Previously served in the "Louisiana Tigers." Enlisted Orange Court House August 18, 1862. Paroled Fairfax Court House May 28, 1865.

Cotterell, P.W. Private, Company B. Place and date of enlistment unknown. Reported sick in a Richmond hospital with pneumonia April 14, 1864. Died April 20, 1864.

Couch, James M. Private, Company C. Previously served in Thirteenth Virginia Infantry. Enlisted Thirty-Ninth Battalion Orange Court House January 11, 1864. Present or accounted for through December 31, 1864. NFR.

Cox, W.R. Private, Company A. Place and date of enlistment unknown. Absent sick in a Richmond hospital with abscess in left jaw September 2, 1864. NFR.

Craddock, David J. Private, Company C. Born 1844. Enlisted Lynchburg October 1, 1862. Reported present or accounted for on surviving muster roll sheets. Paroled Lynchburg April 14, 1865. Died 1912. Interred Spring Hill Cemetery, Lynchburg.

Cristy, Peter. Private, Company B. Enlisted Orange Court House August 18, 1862. Deserted near Madison Court House November 27, 1862.

Cross, Bushrod W. Private, Company A. Born 1847. Enlisted Winchester October 11, 1862. Reported present or accounted for on surviving muster roll sheets. Paroled Edwards Ferry, Maryland, May 5, 1865.

Crostick, J.D. Private, Company C. Place and date of enlistment unknown. Reported in a Richmond hospital May 29, 1864. NFR.

Curren, James. Private, Company B. Place and date of enlistment unknown. Reported AWOL October 1862. NFR.

Cusac, John D. Private, Company A. Born 1834. Previously served in Seventeenth Virginia Infantry. Place and date of enlistment in Thirty-Ninth Battalion unknown. Reported in a Richmond hospital May 20–30, 1864. NFR. Interred Prospect Hill Cemetery, Front Royal.

Daily, Edward. Sergeant, Company B. Enlisted Orange Court House August 18, 1862. Mustered in as private. Reported AWOL October 1862. Returned on unknown date. Promoted to corporal prior to February 1863. Promoted to sergeant May 1, 1863. Paroled Ashland April 1865.

Daniel, Alvis W. Private, Company B. Born 1846. Place and date of enlistment unknown. Reported in a Danville hospital March 23–April 3, 1865, with "Febris Intern Quot." Paroled May 2, 1865. Died 1928. Interred Green Hill Cemetery, Guilford County, North Carolina.

Daniel, William O. Private, Company D. Born 1845. Enlisted Richmond February 18, 1863. NFR.

Davis, Andrew S.T. Private, Company C. Born 1837. Previously served Thirty-First Virginia Infantry. Enlisted in Thirty-Ninth Battalion Staunton December 18, 1862. Reported present or accounted for on surviving muster roll sheets. Paroled Staunton May 23, 1865. Died 1909. Interred Davis Family Cemetery, Highland County.

Davis, John. Private, Company B. Place and date of enlistment unknown. Reported AWOL October 1862.

Demaster, Edward A. Private, Company C. Born 1836. Previously served in Fifth Virginia Infantry. Transferred to Thirty-Ninth Battalion March 26, 1863. Court-martialed for violating Fiftieth Article of War. Present or accounted for through December 1864. Paroled Staunton May 16, 1865. Died 1918. Interred Greenville Baptist Church Cemetery, Staunton.

Demut, Franklin C. Private, Company A. Place and date of enlistment unknown. Reported in a Dalton, Georgia, hospital April 24–30, 1863, with "pleuritis." NFR.

Denny, James W. Private, Company A. Born 1838. Enlisted Williamsport, Maryland, June 26, 1863. Reported present or accounted for on surviving muster roll sheets. Paroled Appomattox Court House April 9, 1865. Died 1923. Interred Loudon Park Cemetery, Baltimore, Maryland.

De Veanning, A.C. Private, Company B. Place and date of enlistment unknown. Reported sick in a Richmond hospital with "cont fever" September 13, 1864. Furloughed September 17, 1864. NFR.

*Dice, P.M. Company unknown.

Dinwiddie, John W. Corporal, Company D. Born 1839. Previously served in Eleventh Virginia Infantry. Enlisted Camp Pickens March 18, 1862. Wounded 1862, place and date unknown. Promoted to corporal prior to September 1864. Paroled Campbell Court House May 27, 1865. Died 1905. Interred Dinwiddie-Cunningham Cemetery, Campbell County.

Dixon, J.P. Private, Company B. Place and date of enlistment unknown. Reported AWOL October 1862.

Dolliff, Abner. Private, Company D. Enlisted Camp Lee November 6, 1862. Reported present or accounted for on surviving muster roll sheets. Paroled Burkesville Junction April 14–17, 1865.

Donnovan, Harrison. Private, Company B. Enlisted Orange Court House August 18, 1862. Present or accounted for until reported absent 1864. NFR.

Douglass, Rice D. Private, Company A. Born 1823. Enlisted Orange Court House August 9, 1863. Reported present or accounted for on surviving muster roll sheets. Paroled Gordonsville April 19, 1865. Died 1904.

Dowdy, James H. Private, Company D. Born 1826. Previously served in Fourth Virginia Cavalry. Enlisted in Thirty-Ninth Battalion at Camp Lee February 18, 1863. Returned to Fourth Virginia Cavalry.

Du Barron, Claude. Corporal, Company C. Born 1845. Enlisted Camp Lee February 18, 1863. Mustered in as a private. Promoted to corporal prior to September 1864. NFR.

Dudley, George. Private, Company A. Enlisted Orange Court House August 21, 1863. Reported AWOL September 27–October 31, 1864. Present November–December 1864. Paroled Appomattox Court House April 9, 1865.

Dudley, John H. Private, Company D. Born 1825. Enlisted Charlottesville August 3, 1863. Detailed as a teamster March 1–December 1, 1864. NFR.

Duke, William B. Private, Company D. Enlisted Goochland County December 20, 1863. Absent sick in a Richmond hospital November 1864–January 4, 1865, with "Int. Fever." NFR.

Dunlap, John C. First Sergeant, Company C. Born 1840. Previously served in Fifth Virginia Infantry. Enlisted Thirty-Ninth Battalion Staunton December 16, 1862. Mustered in as private. Reported sick in a Charlottesville hospital with "debilitas" August 11, 1863. Transferred to a Staunton hospital August 12, 1863. Promoted to sergeant prior to October 1864. Paroled Staunton May 13, 1865.

*Earman, Joseph A. Private, Company B. Born 1845. Died 1900. Interred Green Hill Cemetery, Buena Vista.

Elkins, Presley C. Private, Company D. Born 1831. Previously served in Seventh Virginia Infantry. Enlisted Thirty-Ninth Battalion Rappahannock County July 15, 1863. Reported absent sick in a Danville hospital October 15–24, 1863. Present through December 1864. NFR.

Elliott, George H. Private, Company C. Born 1845. Enlisted Orange Court House January 1, 1864. Reported present or accounted for on surviving muster roll sheets. Paroled Appomattox Court House April 9, 1865. Died 1927. Interred Elliott Cemetery, Albemarle County.

Ellis, James H. Private, Company A. Born 1841. Enlisted Orange Court House January 13, 1864. Reported present or accounted for on surviving muster roll sheets. Paroled Appomattox Court House April 9, 1865. Died 1905.

Ellis, Lewis B. Private, Company A. Enlisted Winchester October 11, 1862. Reported present or accounted for on surviving muster roll sheets. Paroled Appomattox Court House April 9, 1865. Died 1916, Greenville, South Carolina.

Ellis, W.F. Private, Company D. Place and date of enlistment unknown. Reported in a Gordonville hospital with confluent of variola. Died April 13, 1864.

Ellis, William T. Private, Company A. Born 1840. Previously served in Sixth Virginia Cavalry. Transferred to Thirty-Ninth Battalion March 1, 1865. Paroled at Appomattox Court House April 9, 1865. Died 1905, Orange County.

Enwright, Bryan. Private, Company B. Born 1833. Enlisted Richmond October 5, 1862. Reported present or accounted for on surviving muster roll sheets. Paroled Staunton October 3, 1865.

*Eskins, R. Private, Company D.

Eskridge, Charles W. Private, Company A. Born 1842. Enlisted Orange Court House January 15, 1863. Absent Richmond hospital typhoid fever November 29–December 12, 1863. Reported absent without leave December 20, 1864, however, captured Georgetown December 26, 1864. Sent to Point Lookout. Took oath and was released June 11, 1865. Died 1908. Interred Hollywood Cemetery, Richmond.

*Eskridge, Horace P. Private, Company A. Born 1834. Died 1896. Interred Hollywood Cemetery, Richmond.

Estes, Fountain M. Private, Company A. Born 1835. Enlisted Richmond January 30, 1863. Absent Richmond hospital with "Int fever Tirt" August 29, 1864. Furloughed September 6, 1864. Returned to regiment November 11–December 1864. Paroled Louisa Court House May 15, 1865. Died 1906.

*Fahey, Alexander A. Private, company unknown. Born 1842. Enlisted August 1862. Might have also served in the Maryland Line. Died 1883.

Fair, William H. Private, Company C. Previously served in Eighth Virginia Infantry. Enlisted Haymarket September 15, 1862, while AWOL. Present through December 1862. Returned to Eighth Virginia January 3, 1863. Died 1863, Gettysburg, Pennsylvania.

Fanning, J. Private, Company B. Place and date of enlistment unknown. Deserted October 1862.

*Farish, William G. Private, Company B. Born 1847. Died 1931. Interred Riverview Cemetery, Charlottesville.

Farmer, William R. Private, Company C. Born 1843. Previously served in Fifty-Seventh Virginia Infantry. Enlisted Thirty-Ninth Battalion November 20, 1862. Reported present or accounted for on surviving muster roll sheets. Paroled at Appomattox April 9, 1865.

Fiddler, George W. Private, Company A. Born 1838. Enlisted Winchester October 11, 1862. Reported as battalion teamster February 1–December 31, 1864. Paroled Winchester April 21, 1865. Died 1922.

Fiddler, James H. Private, Company A. Enlisted Winchester October 11, 1862. Captured Petersville, Maryland, June 25, 1863. Sent to Fort McHenry. Transferred to Fort Delaware. Died of disease March 9, 1864. Interred Finn's Point, New Jersey.

Fielding, Freeland. Private, Company B. Place and date of enlistment unknown. Reported AWOL August 25, 1862.

Finn, James. Private, Company B. Enlisted Richmond August 18, 1862. Absent sick, "ulcus," November 13, 1862–February 1864. Wounded in action, right leg, October 1864, and admitted to a Charlottesville hospital. Transferred to Lynchburg October 25, 1864. Detailed to work in a Lynchburg hospital March 6, 1865. NFR.

Fisher, Robert H. Private, Company D. Born 1845. Enlisted Richmond February 19, 1863. Absent sick "Fever int tert and acute diarrhoea" October 21–November 5, 1864, in a Richmond hospital. Paroled Burkesville Junction April 14–17, 1865.

Fitch, Samuel B. Private, Company C. Born 1842. Previously served in Fifth Virginia Infantry. Enlisted Thirty-Ninth Battalion December 27, 1862. Reported present or accounted for on surviving muster roll sheets. Paroled Staunton May 20, 1865. Died 1876. Interred Marion, Madison County, Illinois.

Flannagan, John. Corporal, Company B. May have previously served in Fifth Virginia Infantry. Enlisted Thirty-Ninth Battalion Orange Court House August 18, 1862. Captured October 1862 and exchanged. Deserted to the enemy Falls Church September 16, 1864, and sent to Old Capitol Prison. Transferred to Elmira. Released May 17, 1865.

*Fleming, ---. Private, Company B.

*Fletcher, Thomas R. Private, Company E. Died June 22, 1906.

Fletcher, William H. Private, Company A. Born 1830. Enlisted Winchester October 11, 1862. Detailed to Post Office Department October 25, 1862–October 31, 1863. NFR. Died 1892. Interred Fletcher-Rokeby Cemetery, Fauquier County.

Flinn, Eugene H. Private, Company C. Born 1843. Previously served in Dixie Artillery. Enlisted Thirty-Ninth Battalion Luray July 27, 1863. Reported present or accounted for on surviving muster roll sheets. Paroled Appomattox Court House April 9, 1865. Died 1867. Interred Green Hill Cemetery, Page County.

Forsyth, Charles H. Sergeant, Company A. Born 1843. Enlisted Winchester October 11, 1862. Mustered in as corporal. Promoted to sergeant December 1, 1864. Paroled Appomattox Court House April 9, 1865. Died 1922. Interred Mount Hebron Cemetery, Winchester.

Foster, McKendree F. Private, Company A. Born 1845. Previously served in Sixth Virginia Cavalry and Ninth Virginia Cavalry. Enlisted Thirty-Ninth Battalion Orange Court House August 13, 1863. Captured Mine Run November 29, 1863. Sent to Point Lookout, Maryland. Exchanged. Present through December 31, 1864. NFR. Died 1866. Interred Fredericksburg Cemetery, Fredericksburg.

Foster, Warrington D. Private, Company A. Born 1823. Enlisted August 13, 1864. Captured Mine Run September 30, 1863. Sent to Old Capitol Prison. Transferred to Point Lookout prison; exchanged November 15, 1864. Absent through December 31, 1864. NFR. Died 1900. Interred Fredericksburg Cemetery, Fredericksburg.

Franklin, James. Private, Company B. Born 1846. Enlisted Charlottesville August 18, 1862. Absent sick November 27–December 31, 1862, in a hospital near Madison Court House. Reported AWOL January–February 1863. Absent sick with "parolitis" in a Richmond hospital April 19, 1863. Reported in Castle Thunder prison April 24, 1863. Absent sick with "Variola Distinct" in a Richmond hospital May 18–June 16, 1863. Present June 1863. Absent sick August 15–October 31, 1863. Absent on detail as orderly at Belle Island Prison February 3–October 16, 1864. NFR. Died 1908. Interred Fairmont Cemetery, Bedford County.

Franklin, Samuel R. Private, Company C. Born 1843. Previously served in Eighteenth Virginia Infantry. Enlisted Thirty-Ninth Battalion January 11, 1864. Reported present or accounted for on surviving muster roll sheets. NFR. Died 1921. Interred Franklin-Thornton Cemetery, Appomattox County.

Franklin, Thomas E. Private, Company C. Born 1825. Previously served in Sixteenth Virginia Infantry. Enlisted Thirty-Ninth Battalion Orange Court House September 1, 1863. Reported present or accounted for on surviving muster roll sheets. NFR. Died 1900, Lynchburg.

Franklin, W.W. Private, Company B. Place and date of enlistment unknown. Paroled in Virginia May 2, 1865.

Fretwell, John T. Private, Company C. Born 1846. Enlisted Orange Court House January 9, 1864. Absent sick in a Richmond hospital November 1–18, 1864 with "Int fever." Present through December 31, 1864. Paroled Appomattox Court House April 9, 1865. Died 1932. Interred Hillsborough Baptist Church, Albemarle County.

Frye, Phillip F. Private, Company A. Born 1827. Enlisted Winchester November 8, 1862. Reported present or accounted for on surviving muster roll sheets. Paroled Winchester April 20, 1865. Died 1874. Interred St. Paul Cemetery, Frederick County.

Funkhouser, Milton P. Private, Company A. Born 1836. Previously served in Nineteenth Battalion Virginia Artillery and Staunton Local Defense Company. Enlisted Thirty-Ninth Battalion Orange Court House January 1, 1864. Absent sick in hospital April 6–December 31, 1864. Paroled Staunton April 30, 1865. Died 1897. Interred Thornrose Cemetery, Staunton.

Gabbert, David B. Private, Company C. Born 1845. Enlisted Staunton December 16, 1862. Reported present or accounted for on surviving muster roll sheets. Paroled Staunton May 16, 1865. Died 1912. Interred Fairview Cemetery, Buchanan.

Gaines, Pembroke S. Corporal, Company A. Born 1841. Previously served in Fourth Virginia Cavalry. Enlisted Thirty-Ninth Battalion

Winchester November 14, 1862. Mustered in as private. Promoted to corporal September–October 1864. Paroled at Appomattox April 9, 1865. Died 1921. Interred Fauquier County.

Galleher, George G. Private, Company B. Place and date of enlistment unknown. Paroled Edwards Ferry, Maryland, April 29, 1865.

Gander, Martin V.B. Corporal, Company C. Born 1839. Previously served in Dixie Virginia Light Artillery. Enlisted Thirty-Ninth Battalion Luray January 9, 1863. Mustered in as private. Promoted to corporal prior to March 1863. Present through December 1864. NFR. Died 1926. Interred Page County.

Gardner, George W. Private, Company B. Enlisted Haymarket September 14, 1862 Present through October 1863. Paroled Edwards Ferry, Maryland, April 24, 1865.

Garnett, James M. Private, Company D. Born 1847. Enlisted 1865. Paroled Appomattox Court House April 9, 1865. Died 1941. Interred Wingfield Cemetery, Albemarle County.

Garnett, Joel. Private, Company C. Enlisted Orange Court House January 5, 1864. Reported present or accounted for on surviving muster roll sheets. Captured Farmville April 6, 1865. Sent to Point Lookout, Maryland. Released June 11, 1865.

Garnett, John K. Private, Company C. Enlisted Orange Court House August 19, 1863. Reported present or accounted for on surviving muster roll sheets. Paroled Appomattox Court House April 9, 1865.

Garnett, Milton. Private, Company D. Previously served in Nineteenth Virginia Infantry. Transferred to Thirty-Ninth Battalion December 12, 1864. Absent on horse detail December 31, 1864. Paroled at Appomattox Court House April 9, 1865.

Garnett, Robert B. First Sergeant, Company D. Born 1840. Previously served in Fourteenth Virginia Infantry. Enlisted Thirty-Ninth Battalion in Richmond October 15, 1862, as private. Promoted to first sergeant prior to September 1864. Present through December 1864. Paroled

Columbia as private June 1, 1865. Died 1918. Interred Evergreen Cemetery, Galveston, Texas.

Garnett, William F.G., Jr. Private, Company D. Born 1840. Previously served in Richmond Fayette Artillery. Enlisted Thirty-Ninth Battalion January 8, 1864. Absent sick in a Richmond hospital July 5–August 15, 1864 with acute dysentery. Present through December 1864. Paroled in Georgia April 1865.

*Garrison, William. Private, Company A. Born 1844. Died 1932. Interred Restland Memorial Park, Dallas County, Texas.

Gentry, James D. Private, Company C. Born 1846. Enlisted Lynchburg December 1, 1862. Court-martialed for theft but pardoned by President Davis for volunteering in Winder's Legion during Sheridan's May 1864 raid. Present through December 1864. Paroled Amelia Springs May 24, 1865. Died 1926. Interred Hollywood Cemetery, Richmond.

George, Alphonso R. Private, Company D. Born 1844. Enlisted Camp Lee February 18, 1863. Present through September 1, 1863. NFR.

Gibbons, William S. Private, Company C. Born 1842. Previously served as drillmaster, First Tennessee Infantry, and in Tenth Virginia Infantry. Transferred to Thirty-Ninth Battalion May 1864. Captured July 9, 1864, Hedgesville, while scouting. Sent to Wheeling, West Virginia. Transferred to Camp Chase. Exchanged March 2, 1865. NFR. Died 1931. Interred near Rome, Georgia.

Gifford, George. Private, Company B. Enlisted Orange Court House August 18, 1862. Present through February 1862. Transferred to First Battalion Virginia Infantry March–April 1863.

Gilbert, John R. Private, Company D. Enlisted Danville. Present or accounted for through September 1, 1863. NFR.

Gish, James D. Private, Company D. Born 1844. Enlisted Lynchburg October 10, 1862. Present or accounted for through December 1864. NFR. Died 1911. Interred Fairview Cemetery, Roanoke.

Goldsborough, Robert H. Private, Company B. Born 1841. Previously served Chapman's Virginia Battery. Enlisted Thirty-Ninth Battalion Richmond October 29, 1862. Discharged to accept position on staff of General J.E.B. Stuart May 16, 1863. Died of wounds received at Sailors Creek, June 6, 1865. Interred Goldsborough Cemetery, Talbot County, Maryland.

Gordon, Adam H. Private, Company D. Born 1845. Enlisted Orange Court House March 8, 1864. Present through December 1864. Paroled Staunton, Virginia, May 22, 1865.

Gordon, James H. Private, Company C. Previously served in Tenth Virginia Infantry. Enlisted Thirty-Ninth Battalion Luray February 11, 1863, while AWOL. Present or accounted for through February 28, 1863. Reported AWOL through August 31, 1863. Rejoined Tenth Virginia.

Gorrell, James L. Private, Company C. Born 1842. Enlisted Camp Lee February 18, 1863. Captured Martinsburg July 9, 1864. Sent to Wheeling, West Virginia. Transferred to Camp Chase. Exchanged March 12, 1865. NFR.

Goss, Ebenezer. Private, Company D. Born 1820. Previously served in Nineteenth Virginia Infantry. Transferred to Thirty-Ninth Battalion November 23, 1864 in exchange for H.T. McCune. Present through December 1864. Paroled Charlottesville May 17, 1865. Died 1885. Interred Graham Cemetery, Orange County.

Goss, John W. Private, Company D. Previously served in Nineteenth Virginia Infantry. Transferred to Thirty-Ninth Battalion December 12, 1864, in Petersburg. Present through December 31, 1864. NFR.

Green, James R. Private, Company A. Born 1844. Previously served in Sixth Virginia Infantry. Transferred to Thirty-Ninth Battalion March 27, 1864, in Ashland. Reported present or accounted for on surviving muster roll sheets. Paroled Appomattox April 9, 1865. Died 1929. Interred Strother-Green Cemetery, Fauquier County.

Green, Vernon M. Private, Company A. Enlisted Winchester October 11, 1862. Present through July 1863. Died of typhoid fever in a Gordonsville hospital August 12, 1863.

Green, William N. First Lieutenant, Company A. Born 1842. Previously served in Forty-Ninth Virginia Infantry and Thirty-Eighth Battalion Virginia Artillery. Enlisted Thirty-Ninth Battalion Winchester October 11, 1862. Mustered in as first lieutenant. Reported present or accounted for on surviving muster roll sheets. Paroled Appomattox Court House April 9, 1865. Died 1895. Interred Green-Graves Cemetery, Orange County.

Green, William V. First Sergeant, Company A. Born 1842. Enlisted Winchester October 11, 1862. Mustered in as second sergeant. Promoted to first sergeant December 1, 1864. Reported present or accounted for on surviving muster roll sheets. Paroled Winchester May 18, 1865. Interred Prospect Hill Cemetery, Front Royal.

Gregg, Joseph C. Private, Company D. Enlisted Danville May 6, 1863. Reported present or accounted for through December 1864. NFR.

Grim, James M. Private, Company A. Born 1838. Enlisted Winchester October 11, 1862. Reported present or accounted for on surviving muster roll sheets. Paroled at Appomattox Court House April 9, 1865. Died 1887. Interred Files Chapel Cemetery, Frederick County.

Grim, John. Private, Company A. Enlisted Winchester October 11, 1862. Reported present or accounted for on surviving muster roll sheets. Paroled Appomattox Court House April 9, 1865.

*Griscum, George. Adjutant, Field and Staff.

Grover, George. Private, Company B. Enlisted Orange Court House August 8, 1862. Captured and exchanged on unknown date. Absent sick with diarrhea in a Richmond hospital September 10–November 9, 1862. present through March 1864. NFR.

Gruber, William. Private, Company A. Enlisted Winchester October 11, 1862. Deserted November 1, 1862.

*Guerrant, Heran D. Private, Company D.

Hall, James M. Private, Company C. Born 1832. Enlisted Staunton January 6, 1863. Reported AWOL through August 31, 1863. Dropped as a deserter. Died 1912. Interred Calvary Methodist Church Cemetery, Augusta County.

Hall, John W. Private, Company C. Born 1841. Previously served in Fourth Virginia Infantry. Enlisted in Thirty-Ninth Battalion Staunton January 6, 1863. Reported AWOL September 31, 1863, and later dropped as a deserter. Later declared disabled. Died 1904. Interred New Monmouth Presbyterian Church Cemetery, Rockbridge County.

Hall, John W. Private, Company A. Born 1840. Enlisted Fredericksburg November 22, 1862. Present until captured at Gettysburg June 30, 1863. Sent to Chester, Pennsylvania, then paroled. Declared exchanged August 25, 1863. Present through December 31, 1864. Paroled Winchester May 2, 1865. Died 1931. Interred Haislip-Hall Cemetery, Prince William County.

Hall, Lucien D. Private, Company A. Born 1842. Enlisted Winchester October 11, 1862. Captured November 9, 1862, and sent to Old Capitol Prison. Exchanged November 18, 1862. Present or accounted for through December 1864. Paroled Winchester May 2, 1865.

Hamilton, Charles B. Private, Company D. Born 1836. Previously served Seventeenth Virginia Infantry. Detailed as clerk in quartermaster's department. Paroled Winchester April 22, 1865. Died 1881. Interred Ivy Hill Cemetery, Fauquier County.

Hamilton, Eli J. Captain, Quartermaster. Born 1831. Previously served in Sixth Virginia Cavalry. Appointed Field and Staff Thirty-Ninth Battalion August 6, 1863. Present through December 1864. Paroled Appomattox Court House April 9, 1865. Died 1912. Interred Big Ivy Cemetery, Fauquier County.

Hammonds, Thomas B. Private, Company D. Born 1843. Enlisted Winchester October 11, 1862. Captured Prince William County December 9, 1863. Sent to Old Capitol Prison. Transferred to Point Lookout, Maryland. Exchanged November 1, 1864. Absent, horse detail, December 31, 1864. Paroled Appomattox Court House April 9, 1865. Died 1923, Los Angeles, California.

Hand, Thomas, Jr. Private, Company D. Born 1835. Previously served in Seventh Virginia Infantry. Enlisted Thirty-Ninth Battalion, Rappahannock County June 27, 1863. Absent sick in a Richmond hospital October 7–November 10, 1864, with "Feb Remittent." Reported AWOL through December 31, 1864. Paroled Appomattox Court House April 9, 1865.

Hardesty, Lycurgus K. Private, Company A. Born 1845. Enlisted Orange Court House August 17, 1863. Reported present or accounted for on surviving muster roll sheets. Paroled Appomattox Court House April 9, 1865. Died 1922. Interred Elmwood Cemetery, Shepherdstown, West Virginia.

Hargrove, George R. Private, Company D. Previously served in Forty-Fourth Virginia Infantry. Enlisted in Thirty-Ninth Battalion at Camp Lee November 25, 1862. Reported present or accounted for on surviving muster roll sheets. Paroled Richmond April 21, 1865.

Harlow, Catlett M. Private, Company D. Born 1847. Enlisted Orange Court House March 19, 1864. Reported present or accounted for on surviving muster roll sheets. Paroled Louisa Court House May 22, 1865. Died 1885. Interred Lenox Rural Cemetery, Madison County, New York.

Harlow, Joseph C. Private, Company D. Enlisted Orange Court House May 18, 1863. Reported present or accounted for on surviving muster roll sheets. Paroled Appomattox Court House April 9, 1865.

Harmer, John R. Private, Company A. Enlisted Fredericksburg April 16, 1863. Present September–November 1864. Absent on quartermaster detail December 13–31, 1864. Paroled Appomattox Court House April 9, 1865. Died 1908.

*Harnsbarger, Joseph T. Private, Company B. Born 1839. Died 1907. Interred Manassas Cemetery, Manassas.

Harper, George W. Private, Company A. Born 1837. Enlisted Winchester October 11, 1862. Reported present or accounted for through December 31, 1864. NFR. Died 1889. Interred Mount Olive Cemetery, Frederick County.

Harper, Granville H. Private, Company A. Born 1846. Enlisted Winchester October 11, 1862. Absent sick November 18–December 31, 1862. Present January–April 1863. Absent sick August 13, 1862. Present September–December 1864. Paroled Winchester April 25, 1865.

Harper, Samuel H. Quartermaster Sergeant, Field and Staff. Enlisted Lynchburg November 1, 1862, as private, Company C. Promoted to quartermaster sergeant and transferred to Field and Staff prior to September 1864. Reduced to the ranks on December 23, 1864. Present through December 31, 1864. NFR.

Harris, William B., Jr. Private, Company A. Born 1845. Enlisted Williamsport, Maryland, July 13, 1863. Absent on horse detail October 18–31, 1864. Reported AWOL November 6–December 1864. Paroled Winchester April 21, 1865.

Harris, William R. Corporal, Company C. Born 1844. Enlisted Staunton December 16, 1862. Present or accounted for until listed as a deserter March 1864.

Harrison, William L. Private, Company D. Born 1845. Enlisted Richmond January 9, 1863. Admitted to Richmond hospital December 24, 1863. Transferred to a Farmville hospital May 22, 1864, with partial paralysis "caused by typhoid fever." Furloughed for sixty days August 30, 1864. Admitted to a Farmville hospital with "debilitas" April 7, 1865. NFR. Died 1931. Interred Hollywood Cemetery, Richmond.

Hart, Job. Private, Company B. Born 1829. Previously served in Fifth Virginia Infantry. Enlisted Thirty-Ninth Battalion Staunton January 9, 1863. Absent sick in a Richmond hospital September 2, 1864, with "paronychia." Furlough for thirty-five days September 9, 1864. Present November–December 1864. Paroled Appomattox Court House April 9, 1865. Died 1880. Interred Mount Carmel Presbyterian Church Cemetery, Augusta County.

Harvey, Burton. Private, Company D. Born 1836. Previously served in Twentieth Virginia Infantry. Enlisted in Thirty-Ninth Battalion in Richmond February 18, 1863. Present or accounted for through September 1, 1863. Transferred to Eleventh Virginia Infantry.

Harvey, William. Private, Company B. Previously served in Dixie Artillery. Enlisted Thirty-Ninth Battalion August 12, 1862. Reported AWOL September 1, 1863. NFR.

Harvey, William. Private, Company D. Born 1824. Enlisted Camp Lee February 18, 1863. Present through September 1, 1863. NFR.

Hays, Joseph G. Sergeant, Company A. Born 1827. Enlisted Winchester October 11, 1862 as private. Promoted to corporal December 1, 1864. Paroled Winchester May 18, 1865.

Heffley, Joseph P. Private, Company B. Born 1837. Previously served in Weisiger's company and Sixteenth Virginia Infantry. Enlisted Thirty-Ninth Battalion at Winchester May 1, 1862, while AWOL. Absent sick November 1, 1862–October 31, 1863. NFR.

Henderson, Thomas W. Private, Company C. Previously served in Forty-Eighth Virginia Infantry. Enlisted Thirty-Ninth Battalion in Staunton January 1863. Absent sick August 31, 1863. Reported on detached service September–December 1864. Paroled at Appomattox Court House April 9, 1865.

Hereford, James S. Private, Company B. Enlisted Morton's Ford October 6, 1863. Absent sick in hospital October 26–30, 1863. Paroled Campbell Court House May 29, 1865.

*Hierholzer, Alexander. Private, Company C. Born 1833. Died 1896. Interred Holy Cross Cemetery, Richmond.

*Highlander, Thomas. Private, Company B. Born 1844. Died 1921. Interred Oakland Baptist Church, Culpeper County.

*Hinkle, J.A. Company unknown. Enlisted Nelson County April 1, 1862. NFR.

Hite, Henry C. Private, Company D. Born 1845. Previously served in Dixie Artillery and Cayce's Artillery. Transferred to Thirty-Ninth Battalion January 9, 1863. Reported present or accounted for on surviving muster rolls. Paroled at Appomattox April 9, 1865. Died 1926. Interred Thornrose Cemetery, Staunton.

Hite, Isaac M. Private, Company C. Born 1835. Place and date of enlistment unknown. Paroled Appomattox Court House April 9, 1865. Died 1898. Interred New Lebanon Cumberland Presbyterian Church Cemetery, Cooper County, Missouri.

*Hite, John M. Private, Company A. Born 1840. Died 1914. Interred Mount Carmel Presbyterian Church Cemetery, Augusta County.

Hite, Marion M. Private, Company A. Born 1821. Enlisted Orange Court House October 1, 1863. Detailed to Army of Northern Virginia Headquarters. Absent sick, "debilitas," in a Richmond hospital October 19–22, 1864. Paroled Appomattox Court House April 9, 1865. Died 1902. Interred Mount Paran Baptist Church Cemetery, Nelson County.

Hodges, John W. Private, Company A. Enlisted Winchester October 11, 1862. Present through August 31, 1863. NFR.

Hodgson, Abner W. Private, Company A. Enlisted Winchester October 11, 1862. Present through August 31, 1863. Absent sick in a Richmond hospital June 15–August 3, 1864 with "Cont. fever." Present through December 1864. NFR.

Hoffman, Thomas W. Private, Company B. Previously served in Second Virginia Infantry. Enlisted Thirty-Ninth Battalion Orange Court House August 18, 1862. Present through February 1863. Transferred to Seventeenth Virginia Infantry April 9, 1863.

Hooper, Judson V. Private, Company A. Born 1846. Enlisted Winchester October 11, 1862. Absent sick in a Charlottesville hospital August 9, 1863 with "debilitas." Transferred to a Richmond hospital September 2, 1863. Present September–December 1864. Paroled Appomattox Court House April 9, 1865. Died 1916. Interred Fairview Cemetery, Roanoke.

Houck, Charles W. Private, Company A. Born 1837. Enlisted Winchester October 11, 1862. Reported present or accounted for on surviving muster rolls. Paroled at Appomattox Court House April 9, 1865. Died 1913 at Winchester.

House, Nathaniel B. Private, Company A. Born 1829. Enlisted Prince William County October 6, 1863. Reported present or accounted for on surviving muster rolls. Paroled Fairfax Court House April 28, 1865. Died 1901. Interred Greenwich Presbyterian Church Cemetery, Prince William County.

Hughes, Elisha W. Private, Company D. Born 1847. Enlisted Camp Lee February 18, 1863. NFR.

Hunter, George D.M. Private, Company A. Born 1844. Enlisted Orange Court House January 23, 1864. Reported present or accounted for until AWOL December 30–31, 1864. Paroled Louisa Court House May 15, 1865. Died 1924. Interred Oakland Cemetery, Louisa County.

Hunter, H.C. Private, Company B. Place and date of enlistment unknown. Reported AWOL October 1862–January 1, 1863. NFR.

Hunter, Thomas E. Private, Company C. Born 1823. Previously served in Thirteenth Virginia Infantry. Enlisted in Thirty-Ninth Battalion Lynchburg January 12, 1863. Reported present or accounted for on surviving muster rolls. Paroled Campbell Court House May 30, 1865. Died 1891.

Hunter, T.R. Private, Company D. Enlisted Greenwich July 6, 1863. NFR.

Huntsberry, Jacob A. Private, Company A. Born 1844. Enlisted Winchester October 11, 1862. Transferred to Twelfth Virginia Cavalry April 22, 1863. Died 1913. Interred Lutheran Reformed Church Cemetery, New Market.

Hutchinson, James. Private, Company B. Enlisted Orange County August 18, 1862. Present or accounted for through April 30, 1863. Reported AWOL through October 31, 1863. NFR.

Hutchison, Westwood. Private, Company B. Born 1846. Enlisted Petersburg August 17, 1864. Paroled Fairfax Court House June 1, 1865. Died 1933. Interred Hutchison Cemetery, Prince William County.

Iden, John N. Private, Company A. Born 1840. Previously served in Fauquier Artillery. Enlisted Thirty-Ninth Battalion Winchester October 11,

1862. Absent serving in Stribling's Battery October 20, 1862–August 31, 1863. Captured Suffolk April 19, 1863. Sent to Fort Monroe. Exchanged April 1863. Present through February 1865. Paroled Millwood April 20, 1865. Died 1890. Interred Ivy Hill Cemetery, Upperville.

Jackson, Andrew J. Private, Company A. Previously served in First Maryland Infantry. Enlisted Thirty-Ninth Battalion Richmond February 18, 1863. Transferred to First Maryland Cavalry December 17, 1863.

Jackson, Evander J. Private, Company D. Enlisted Charlottesville June 30, 1863. Reported present or accounted for until absent sick November–December 1864. NFR.

Jackson, James A. Private, Company D. Born 1847. Enlisted Camp Lee February 19, 1863. Present through September 1, 1863. NFR.

Jackson, James A. Private, Company D. Previously served in Thirty-Eighth Virginia Infantry. Enlisted Thirty-Ninth Battalion Danville June 7, 1863. Reported present or accounted for until absent sick September–December 1864. NFR.

Jackson, John W. First Lieutenant, Company D. Born 1842. Previously served in Twentieth Virginia Infantry. Enlisted Thirty-Ninth Battalion 1863. Elected second lieutenant January 26, 1864. Promoted to first lieutenant March 9, 1864. Absent sick in a Richmond hospital November 5, 1864, with "Febris Remit." Paroled Richmond April 28, 1865. Died 1929. Interred Jackson Cemetery, Fluvanna County.

Jacobs, Richard S. Private, Company D. Born 1839. Enlisted Culpeper Court House April 15, 1863. Reported absent on detached service with General Early September–December 1864. Paroled Fairfax Court House May 9, 1865. Died 1909. Interred Mitchells Presbyterian Church Cemetery, Orange County.

James, Robert L. Private, Company C. Born 1839. Enlisted Culpeper Court House July 20, 1863. Reported absent sick August 1863 and September 12–February 3, 1864. Paroled Guyandotte April 1865.

Javins, W.F. Private, Company D. Born 1846. Enlisted Greenwich July 6, 1863. NFR. Died 1872. Interred St. Paul's Episcopal Church Cemetery, Alexandria.

Jenkins, Christian. Private, Company, C. Enlisted Luray March 1, 1863. Reported AWOL through April 30, 1863. Present May–August 1863. Court-martialed December 29, 1863. Absent serving sentence February 1, 1864–October 1864. Present November–December 1864. Transferred to Twenty-Eighth Virginia Infantry January 6, 1865.

*Jenkins, David C. Private, company unknown. Born 1846. Died 1909. Interred Thornrose Cemetery, Staunton.

Jenkins, William H. Private, Company C. Born 1843. Previously served in Pegram's Battery. Transferred to Thirty-Ninth Battalion Luray January 9, 1863. Reported present or accounted for until absent on detached service with Gen. A.P. Hill, September–December 1864. Paroled Appomattox April 9, 1865. Died 1908. Interred Ladoga Cemetery, Montgomery County, Indiana.

Jennings, Leonard H. Private, Company B. Enlisted Orange Court House August 18, 1862. Mustered in as corporal. Reduced to ranks April 30, 1864. Reported captured July 3–5, 1863; however, Federal records do not substantiate this claim. NFR.

Job, Harrison. Private, Company C. Enlisted Luray February 1, 1863. Reported present or accounted for on surviving muster rolls until transferred to Fifth Virginia Cavalry March 1, 1865. Died 1914. Interred Newport, Page County.

Johns, Joshua O. Private, Company C. Enlisted Orange Court House December 21, 1863. Reported present or accounted for on surviving muster rolls. Paroled Appomattox April 9, 1865.

Johnson, Norborne T. Private, Company C. Born 1845. Enlisted Orange Court House January 1, 1864. Present on surviving muster rolls until reported absent on horse detail December 24–31, 1864. Captured Richmond April 10, 1865. Confined in Libby prison. NFR. Died 1902. Interred Thornrose Cemetery, Staunton.

Jones, Edmund W. Private, Company C. Born 1834. Enlisted Orange Court House January 19, 1864. Absent detailed as clerk, Army of Northern Virginia headquarters, August 31, 1864–December 31, 1864. Paroled Lynchburg April 15, 1865. Died 1896. Interred Spring Hill Cemetery, Lynchburg.

Jones, John T. Private, Company C. Born 1832. Enlisted Lynchburg November 1, 1862. Present or accounted for on surviving muster rolls. Paroled Campbell Court House June 1, 1865. Died 1903. Presbyterian Cemetery, Lynchburg.

Jones, Thomas W. Private, Company C. Enlisted Richmond November 1, 1862. Reported AWOL through August 31, 1863. Dropped as a deserter. Died 1883. Interred Spring Hill Cemetery, Lynchburg.

Jones, William T. Private, Company B. Born 1835. Previously served in unknown Confederate regiment. Enlisted Thirty-Ninth Battalion Orange Court House August 18, 1862. Absent sick in a Guinea hospital January 8–April 1863 and as a smallpox nurse May 31, 1863. Present July–October 1863. Absent sick in a Richmond hospital February 7–8, 1864. Transferred to Callaway's Georgia Battery July 5, 1864.

Jordan, J.W. Private, Company D. Enlisted Camp Lee January 1, 1863. Reported present or accounted for on surviving muster rolls through June 30, 1863. NFR.

Jordan, James. Private, Company B. Enlisted Orange Court House August 18, 1862. Deserted near Madison Court House November 27, 1862. NFR.

Judd, Benjamin E. Private, Company D. Born 1844. Enlisted Rappahannock County June 4, 1863. Present on surviving muster rolls until reported AWOL November 1864. NFR. Died 1916. Interred Judd Cemetery, Page County.

Judd, T. Wallace. Private, Company D. Enlisted Middleburg June 15, 1863. Present or accounted for through June 30, 1863. NFR.

Kackley, Elias A. Private, Company A. Born 1822. Enlisted Fredericksburg April 1, 1863. Reported as Battalion teamster February 1–December 31, 1864. NFR. Died 1902. Interred Gravel Springs Cemetery, Frederick County.

Kaufman, Carl. Private, Company B. Born 1826. Enlisted Staunton October 27, 1862. Transferred to First Maryland Cavalry April 21, 1864.

Kaufman, John B. Private, Company A. Born 1845. Enlisted Orange Court House January 1, 1864. Absent sick in a Richmond hospital August 25, 1864, with "fever remit." Transferred to a Staunton hospital August 29, 1864. Present September–December 1864. Paroled Winchester April 19, 1865. Died 1908 in Philadelphia, Pennsylvania.

Keller, Jacob F. Private, Company C. Born 1829. Previously served Forty-Sixth Virginia Infantry. Enlisted Thirty-Ninth Battalion Staunton December 16, 1862. Detailed as teamster November 1863–January 1864. Reported present until absent on horse detail December 24–31, 1864. Paroled Staunton May 12, 1865.

Keller, John. Private, Company A. Enlisted Winchester October 11, 1862. AWOL November 19, 1862. Dropped as deserter.

Kennedy, George W. Private, Company C. Born 1844. Previously served Fifty-Second Virginia Infantry. Enlisted Thirty-Ninth Battalion Staunton February 15, 1863. Reported AWOL through August 31, 1863. Reported as courier for General Early December 8, 1864. NFR. Died 1926. Interred Crown Hill Cemetery, Clifton Forge.

Kent, Daniel M. Ordnance Sergeant, Field and Staff. Enlisted Stone Bridge November 6, 1862, as a private in Company B. Captured Annapolis, Maryland, April 18, 1863. Sent to Fort McHenry. Exchanged May 1863. Promoted to sergeant September 1, 1863. Absent sick in a Richmond hospital November 2–December 13, 1863 with "Feb. remit." Appointed ordnance sergeant May 4, 1864, and transferred to Field and Staff. Present through December 1864. Paroled Ashland April 26, 1865.

*Kent, H. Bland. Major, Field and Staff.

Kern, Hamilton. Private, Company A. Enlisted Winchester October 11, 1862. Absent sick October 25, 1862. Died November 1862.

Kerr, John M. Private, Company C. Born 1840. Enlisted Orange Court House December 8, 1863. Reported AWOL October 4–31, 1864. Present November–December 1864. Paroled Staunton May 16, 1865.

Kerr, Robert B. Private, Company C. Born 1844. Previously served Fifth Virginia Infantry. Enlisted Thirty-Ninth Battalion Staunton December 15, 1862. Discharged for epilepsy May 31, 1863.

Kerr, William S. Private, Company C. Born 1841. Previously served in Fifty-Second Virginia Infantry. Transferred to Thirty-Ninth Battalion May 1, 1863, in exchange for John Spillman. Reported present or accounted for on surviving muster rolls. Paroled Staunton May 3, 1865. Died 1875. Interred Shemariah Church Cemetery, Augusta County.

King, George W. Private, Company D. Enlisted Danville June 20, 1863. Transferred to Thirty-Eighth Virginia Infantry in exchange for Christopher Carter December 1, 1864.

King, William B. Private, Company B. Place and date of enlistment unknown. Paroled Louisa Court House May 15, 1865.

Kinnier, James O. Private, Company C. Born 1843. Previously served in Eleventh Virginia Infantry. Enlisted Thirty-Ninth Battalion Orange Court House January 9, 1864. Captured Martinsburg July 9, 1864, and sent to Wheeling, West Virginia. Transferred to Camp Chase. Exchanged March 12, 1865. Reported in a Richmond hospital with "diarrhoea" March 13, 1865. Furloughed March 17, 1865. Paroled Lynchburg April 13, 1865. Died 1904. Interred Presbyterian Cemetery, Roanoke.

Kirtley, Robert F. Private, Company C. Enlisted Orange Court House September 26, 1863. Reported present or accounted for on surviving muster rolls. Paroled Appomattox Court House April 9, 1865.

Kite, William H. Private, company unknown. Previously served in Nineteenth Virginia Infantry. Transferred to Thirty-Ninth Battalion October 30, 1864. NFR.

*Kloman, Edward F. Private, company unknown. Born 1838. Died 1917. Interred Warrenton Cemetery, Warrenton.

Knight, Henry. Private, Company C. Enlisted Luray March 1, 1863. Reported AWOL through April 30, 1863. Present through August 13, 1863. Court-martialed for desertion January 27, 1864. Deserted July 8, 1864.

Knipple, Edward B. Corporal, Company C. Previously served in Tenth Virginia Infantry. Enlisted Thirty-Ninth Battalion Staunton December 16, 1862, as corporal. Transferred back to Tenth Virginia prior to May 12, 1864. Died 1916. Interred Linville Brethren Church Cemetery, Rockingham County.

Koiner, George M.K. Private, Company C. Born 1841. Previously served in Fifty-Second Virginia Infantry. Enlisted Thirty-Ninth Battalion Orange Court House January 20, 1864. Reported present or accounted for on surviving muster rolls. Paroled Staunton May 17, 1865. Died 1912. Interred Trinity Lutheran Cemetery, Waynesboro.

Koontz, John M. Private, Company A. Born 1840. Enlisted Winchester October 11, 1862. Fined for lost items. Paroled Appomattox Court House April 9, 1865. Died 1908. Interred Keezletown Cemetery, Rockingham County.

Koontz, William F. Private, Company A. Born 1834. Enlisted Winchester October 11, 1862. Reported present or accounted for on surviving muster rolls. Fined for lost items. NFR. Died 1918. Interred Keezletown Cemetery, Rockingham County.

Lannean, Hudson. Private, Company C. Enlisted Richmond March 9, 1863. Reported AWOL August 31, 1863. Dropped as deserter.

Larkin, Pat. Private, Company B. Place and date of enlistment unknown. Reported AWOL October 1862. NFR.

Larkin, Thomas N. Private, Company D. Born 1842. Enlisted Camp Lee October 1, 1862. Reported present or accounted for on surviving muster rolls through December 31, 1864. NFR. Died 1913. Interred Spring Hill Cemetery, Lynchburg.

Laws, Benjamin R. Private, Company A. Born 1835. Enlisted Winchester October 11, 1862. Present or accounted for until reported sick in a Richmond hospital January 18–September 8, 1864, with "remit fever." Present through December 31, 1864. Paroled Fairfax Court House May 12, 1865.

Laws, Bushrod M. Private, Company A. Born 1841. Enlisted Oakley Springs March 3, 1863. Court-martialed August 1864. Absent in a Winchester hospital November 23–December 31, 1864. Paroled Winchester April 22, 1865.

Laws, John W. Corporal, Company A. Enlisted Winchester October 11, 1862 as corporal. Died in a Staunton hospital of typhoid fever January 3 or May 5, 1864. Interred Thornrose Cemetery, Lynchburg.

Leavel, Thomas F. Private, Company D. Born 1835. Enlisted Culpeper Court House June 15, 1863. Absent sick in a Richmond hospital June 30, 1864, with gonorrhea. Furloughed August 2, 1864. Present though December 31, 1864. Paroled Mount Jackson April 20, 1865. Died 1880. Interred Friedens Church Cemetery, Rockingham County.

Lee, Ludwell. Private, Company A. Born 1846. Enlisted Winchester October 11, 1862. Reported present or accounted for on surviving muster rolls. Paroled Appomattox Court House April 9, 1865. Died 1909. Interred Ivy Hill Cemetery, Upperville.

*Lee, Vernon. Private, company unknown.

Lehew, Jonathan B. Corporal, Company A. Born 1829. Enlisted Winchester October 11, 1862, as corporal. Acting commissary sergeant November–December 1864. Paroled Winchester May 16, 1865. Died 1908. Interred Prospect Hill Cemetery, Front Royal.

Lemar, Eugune F. Private, Company C. Enlisted Richmond May 1, 1863. Reported AWOL through August 31, 1863. Dropped as deserter.

*Lewis, J.W. Private, company unknown. Interred Thornrose Cemetery, Staunton.

Lines, James K.P. Private, Company C. Born 1844. Enlisted Staunton February 15, 1863. Court-martialed March 8, 1864, for violating Fiftieth

Article of War. Present or accounted for through December 31, 1864. Paroled Staunton May 10, 1865.

Lionberger, John H. First Lieutenant, Company C. Born 1843. Previously served in Seventh Virginia Cavalry and Dixie Artillery. Transferred to Thirty-Ninth Battalion March 14, 1863 as first lieutenant. Reported present or accounted for on surviving muster rolls through December 31, 1864. NFR. Died 1879. Interred Green Hill Cemetery, Luray.

Lithgow, William T. Private, Company B. Born 1826. Enlisted Orange Court House August 18, 1862. Detailed as clerk in C.S. Ambulance Works, Richmond, October 14, 1864. NFR.

Littlejohn, William W. Private, Company B. Place and date of enlistment unknown. Detailed as messenger, courier or clerk, inspector general's office, March 9, 1863–August 1864. Paroled at Appomattox Court House April 9, 1865.

Locke, John H. Private, Company A. Previously served in Sixth Virginia Cavalry. Enlisted Thirty-Ninth Battalion Winchester October 11, 1862, without permission. Transferred back to Sixth Virginia November 1863.

Lockridge, William H. Private, Company C. Enlisted Orange Court House February 7, 1864. Present on surviving muster rolls through December 31, 1864. NFR.

Loomis, Henry. Private, Company B. Enlisted Orange Court House August 18, 1862. Transferred to Thirty-Eighth Mississippi March 9, 1863.

Lovell, William S. Private, Company C. Born 1848. Enlisted Orange Court House January 20, 1864. Present through January 31, 1864. Paroled Appomattox Court House April 9, 1865. Died 1883. Interred Lovell Cemetery, Frederick County.

Lowe, Rector. Private, Company A. Born 1839. Enlisted Winchester October 11, 1862. Deserted November 5, 1862. Died 1899. Interred Andrews Chapel Cemetery, Fairfax County.

Lowman, James D. Private, Company A. Born 1836. Enlisted Staunton January 6, 1863. Reported AWOL through August 31, 1863. Dropped as a deserter. Died 1913. Interred Windy Cove Presbyterian Church Cemetery, Bath County.

Lupton, James F. Private, Company A. Previously served in Thirteenth Virginia Infantry. Transferred to Thirty-Ninth Battalion January 27, 1863. Absent sick in a Richmond hospital September 16–October 20, 1864. Present November–December 1864. Captured Cedar Creek March 7, 1865, and sent to Fort McHenry. Released May 1, 1865. Interred Confederate Memorial Cemetery, Missouri.

Lupton, John C. Private, Company A. Enlisted Culpeper Court House July 24, 1863. Absent sick in a Richmond hospital July 20, 1864. Died of typhoid fever and chronic "diarrhoea" July 29, 1864.

*Lupton, John H. Private, Company A. Born 1846. Died 1924. Interred Thornrose Cemetery, Staunton.

Lupton, John M. Private, Company A. Born 1841. Enlisted Winchester October 11, 1862. Absent sick in a Richmond hospital September–October 1863. Present September–December 1864. Paroled Winchester April 20, 1864. Died 1902. Interred Mount Hebron Cemetery, Winchester.

Lupton, John R. Sergeant, Company A. Born 1842. Enlisted Winchester October 1, 1862. Mustered in as sergeant. Absent sick in a Richmond hospital October 10–14, 1863, with "Fevar Int. tert." Absent sick in a Staunton hospital January 21–February 29, 1864, with "diarrhoea." Absent sick in a Richmond hospital September 19–October 14, 1864, with "diarrhoea." Paroled Appomattox Court House April 9, 1865. Died 1913. Interred Woodlawn Cemetery, Harrisonburg.

Lupton, Joseph M. Private, Company A. Born 1842. Enlisted Winchester October 11, 1862. Reported present or accounted for on surviving muster rolls. Paroled Winchester April 24, 1865. Died 1909. Interred Frederick County.

Lupton, Joshua S. Private, Company A. Born 1820. Enlisted Winchester October 11, 1862. On detail as wagon master, army headquarters, February

12, 1863–December 1864. Paroled Appomattox Court House April 9, 1865. Died 1904, Loudoun County.

Lupton, Josiah L.F. Second Lieutenant, Company A. Born 1842. Enlisted Winchester October 11, 1862. Mustered in as second lieutenant. Detailed as battalion adjutant May–August 1863. Present September–December 1864. Paroled Winchester April 24, 1865.

Lupton, Thomas G. Private, Company A. Born 1843. Enlisted Winchester October 11, 1862. Reported present or accounted for on surviving muster rolls. Paroled Appomattox Court House April 9, 1865. Died 1926. Interred Mount Hebron Cemetery, Winchester.

Marks, Thomas M. Assistant Surgeon, Field and Staff. Born 1838. Previously served in Ninth Louisiana Infantry. Appointed to Thirty-Ninth Battalion June 3, 1863. Reported present or accounted for on surviving muster rolls. Paroled at Appomattox Court House April 9, 1865. Died 1900. Interred Greenwood Cemetery, Harrison County, Texas.

Marlow, ---. Private, Company D. Enlisted Danville August 25, 1863. NFR.

*Marshall, Ralph A. Private, Company B.

Mason, Landon R. First Sergeant, Company B. Born 1843. Previously served in Seventeenth Virginia Infantry. Enlisted Thirty-Ninth Battalion Haymarket September 17, 1862. Absent sick November 25–December 31, 1862. Discharged by reason of disability April 23, 1863. Died 1923. Interred Hollywood Cemetery, Richmond.

Mays, George B. Private, Company D. Born 1845. Enlisted Richmond February 18, 1863. Present June 1–September 1, 1863. NFR.

McArtor, Thomas W. Private, Company A. Born 1836. Previously served in Sixth Virginia Cavalry. Transferred Thirty-Ninth Battalion February 14, 1864. Present September–December 1864. NFR. Died 1911. Interred Stephens City, Frederick County.

*McCarthy, James. Private, Company A.

McCune, Henson T. Private, Company D. Born 1820. Previously served in Thirty-Eighth Virginia Infantry. Enlisted Thirty-Ninth Battalion Danville August 18, 1863. Present September–October 1864. Transferred to Nineteenth Virginia Infantry November 3, 1864. Died 1896. Interred Bassett Cemetery, Henry County.

McCune, Thomas C. Private, Company D. Enlisted Danville June 10, 1863. Present through September 1, 1863. NFR.

McCune, William. Private, Company D. Enlisted Danville November 16, 1863. Present until transferred to Nineteenth Virginia Infantry December 1864.

McDonald, Josiah. Private, Company A. Born 1840. Enlisted Winchester October 11, 1862. Court-martialed March 19, 1863. Reported present or accounted for on surviving muster rolls through September 1864. NFR. Died 1927. Interred Green Hill Cemetery, Berryville.

McGrouth, James. Private, Company C. Enlisted Richmond April 14, 1863, as substitute for James R. Mountcastle. Deserted April 1863.

McKaig, John V.B. Private, Company D. Enlisted Richmond March 10, 1863. Captured Williamsport, Maryland, July 14, 1863. Sent to Point Lookout, Maryland. Exchanged May 8, 1864. Reported AWOL September–December 1864. NFR.

McKaig, Thomas J., Jr. First Lieutenant, Company D. Born 1840. Promoted to second lieutenant Thirty-Ninth Battalion Danville January 26, 1864. Promoted to first lieutenant March 9, 1864. Absent sick in a Richmond hospital September 23–October 4, 1864, with "chronic diarrheoa." Returned to company November–December 1864. Paroled Greensboro, North Carolina, May 1, 1865. Died 1886. Interred Rose Hill Cemetery, Allegany County, Maryland.

McKinley, Merchant M. Private, Company D. Enlisted Camp Lee November 1, 1862. Reported present or accounted for on surviving muster rolls. Paroled at Appomattox Court House April 9, 1865.

*McPheeters, William. Private, Company C.

McPheethers, Robert. Private, Company C. Born 1845. Enlisted Orange Court House November 1, 1863. Absent on horse detail December 24–31, 1864. Paroled Staunton May 15, 1865. Died 1921. Interred Bethel Presbyterian Church Cemetery, Augusta County.

Mewburn, Nathaniel J. Private, Company D. Born 1843. Previously served in First Maryland Infantry. Enlisted Thirty-Ninth Battalion Camp Lee February 18, 1863. Reported present or accounted for on surviving muster rolls. Paroled Danville May 1, 1865. Died 1917. Interred Woodbine Cemetery, Harrisonburg.

Middleton, David C. Private, Company C. Born 1844. Previously served in Dixie Artillery. Enlisted Thirty-Ninth Battalion February 1, 1863. Captured Strasburg October 19, 1864. Sent to a Baltimore hospital. Took oath and was released February 7, 1865.

Milhorn, Joseph H. Bugler, Company A. Born 1827. Previously served in Second Virginia Infantry. Enlisted Thirty-Ninth Battalion October 11, 1862 as private. Promoted chief bugler prior to September 1864. Present through December 1864. Paroled Appomattox April 9, 1865. Died 1898, Kansas City, Missouri.

*Miller, Albert C. Private, Company A.

Miller, Albert L. Private, Company A. Enlisted Winchester October 11, 1862. Present through August 13, 1863. AWOL through December 1864. NFR.

Miller, Albert P. Sergeant, Company B. Born 1845. Place and date of enlistment unknown. Paroled Winchester May 10, 1865. Died 1922. Interred Masonic Cemetery, Grundy County, Missouri.

Miller, John. Private, Company A. Born 1833. Enlisted Middleburg June 28, 1863. Present or accounted for through June 30, 1863. Deserted Martinsburg November 4, 1863. Sent to Fort Mifflin, Pennsylvania. Escaped January 19, 1864. NFR. Died 1910. Interred Morning Star Church Cemetery, Luray.

Miller, William F. Private, Company C. Born 1838. Enlisted Luray January 10, 1863. Detailed as battalion teamster November 1, 1863–December 31, 1864. Surrendered Appomattox Court House April 9, 1865. Died 1895. Interred Rockland Community Cemetery, Page County.

Mitchell, ---. Private, Company D. Enlisted Danville July 15, 1863. Present or accounted for through September 1, 1863. NFR.

*Mitchell, Frederick. Second Lieutenant, Company C.

Mohler, Henry N. Private, Company C. Born 1845. Enlisted Orange County September 1, 1863. Absent on detached duty Drewy's Bluff September–October 1864. Present November–December 1864. NFR.

Moneymaker, Eli C. Private, Company C. Born 1824. Previously served in Fifth Virginia Infantry. Enlisted Thirty-Ninth Battalion Staunton March 1, 1863 without authority. Present through August 31, 1863. Returned to Fifth Virginia October 1863. Died 1907. Interred Union Presbyterian Church Cemetery, Augusta County.

Moore, James F. Private, Company B. Place and date of enlistment unknown. Paroled Louisa Court House May 15, 1865.

Moore, William F. Private, Company B. Place and date of enlistment unknown. Paroled Greensboro, North Carolina, May 5, 1865.

Moran, Edward. Private, company unknown. Place and date of enlistment unknown. Detailed as a teamster May–November 1864. NFR.

Morris, William G. Private, Company A. Born 1832. Enlisted Winchester October 11, 1862. Present through August 31, 1863. Transferred to Sixth Virginia Cavalry February 10, 1864.

Morrison, Thomas J. Private, Company D. Previously served in Fifty-Seventh Virginia Infantry. Enlisted Thirty-Ninth Battalion May 29, 1863. Absent sick in Richmond with "Int Fev" October 24–November 2, 1864. Present through December 31, 1864. NFR.

Morton, George W. Private, Company A. Born 1845. Enlisted Fredericksburg April 1, 1863. Reported present or accounted for on surviving muster rolls through December 1864. NFR. Died 1918. Interred North Pamunkey Church Cemetery, Orange County.

Morton, Thomas. Corporal, Company B. Born 1832. Previously served in First Virginia Cavalry. Enlisted Charlottesville August 18, 1862, as corporal. Present or account for until transferred to Maryland Line March 31, 1864.

Mount, Charles E.A. Second Lieutenant, Company B. Born 1828. Previously served 132nd Virginia Militia. Enlisted Thirty-Ninth Battalion Orange Court House August 18, 1862. Present or accounted for until reported wounded and in a Charlottesville hospital January 31–April 27, 1864. Present May 1, 1864, through February 1, 1865. Paroled Fairfax Court House April 22, 1865. Died 1890. Interred Sharon Cemetery, Loudoun County.

Mountcastle, James R. Private, Company C. Enlisted Richmond April 13, 1863. Furnished James McGrouth as substitute and discharged April 14, 1863.

Mudd, George L. Corporal, Company B. Enlisted Richmond October 29, 1862. Promoted to corporal May 1, 1863. Paroled Richmond April 26, 1865.

*Murfree, Benjamin T. Private, Company C.

Murray, Patrick P. Private, Company D. Born 1845. Enlisted Camp Lee October 2, 1862. Absent on detached service in a Lynchburg hospital September–October 1864. Absent with double hernia in a Richmond hospital November 11, 1865. Discharged January 15, 1865.

Myers, Austin G. Corporal, Company C. Born 1842. Previously served in Thirty-First Virginia Infantry. Transferred to Thirty-Ninth Battalion November 11, 1862. Mustered in as a corporal. Absent sick March–April 1865. Reported AWOL September 12, 1864. Wounded and captured at Beverly October 29, 1864. Sent to Camp Chase then transferred to Point Lookout. Released June 21, 1865.

Nelson, W.E. Private, company unknown. Place and date of enlistment unknown. Took oath in Richmond May 16, 1865.

*Nichols, Robert J. First Lieutenant, Company C. Oklahoma.

Norman, Henry C. Private, Company B. Born 1845. Place and date of enlistment unknown. Paroled Appomattox Court House April 9, 1865. Died 1906. Interred Oak Ridge Cemetery, South Boston.

*Opie, John W. Captain, Company E.

Orndorff, Ananias. Private, Company A. Born 1843. Enlisted Winchester October 11, 1862. Deserted November 19, 1862. Later served in Eleventh Virginia Cavalry. Died 1925. Interred St. James Cemetery, Shenandoah County.

Orndorff, George F. Private, Company D. Enlisted Winchester October 11, 1862. Deserted November 19, 1862.

Orr, Henry S. Private, Company B. Place and date of enlistment unknown. Reported AWOL September 20, 1863.

*Overton, Moses. Private, company unknown. Place and date of enlistment unknown. Reported in Castle Thunder prison February 8, 1863. NFR.

Owens, Somers J. Private, Company B. Enlisted Richmond September 30, 1862. Absent on leave March 26, 1863. Reported AWOL through June 30, 1863. Present September–October 1863. Died of apoplexy, Gordonsville Hospital, November 11, 1863.

Page, Carter. Private, Company D. Born 1843. Previously served Twentieth Virginia Infantry. Enlisted Thirty-Ninth Battalion Camp Lee September 25, 1862. Reported wounded in action in left leg and captured. However, admitted to a Richmond hospital June 12, 1863. Released as paroled prisoner June 17, 1863. NFR. Died 1910. Interred Union Cemetery, Loudoun County.

*Page, Charles H. Private, Company C. Born 1837. Previously served in Eleventh Virginia Infantry. Transferred to Thirty-Ninth Battalion December 17, 1862. NFR. Died 1901. Interred Hollywood Cemetery, Richmond.

Page, Oscar D. Private, Company D. Enlisted Orange Court House June 15, 1863. Reported AWOL September 1864. NFR.

Page, William H. Private, Company C. Enlisted Richmond or Luray May 1, 1863. Absent sick in Richmond with dysentery July 16, 1864. Present through December 31, 1864. NFR.

Page, William W. Captain, Company D. Born 1840. Previously served in Twentieth Virginia Infantry. Raised cavalry company, which was assigned to Thirty-Ninth Battalion September 30, 1863. Present or accounted for on surviving rolls until absent on furlough November–December 1864. NFR. Died 1920. Interred Mount Hope Cemetery, Westchester, New York.

Palmer, C.L. Private, Company D. Place and date of enlistment unknown. Paroled Farmville April 11–21, 1865.

Palmore, Frederick J. Private, Company D. Born 1845. Enlisted Camp Lee February 18, 1863. Reported present or accounted for on surviving muster rolls. Paroled Farmville April 11–21, 1865. Died 1888. Interred Springfield National Cemetery, Springfield, Missouri.

Panill, John B. Private, Company C. Born 1844. Enlisted Orange Court House October 3, 1863. Absent sick April 26–October 31, 1864. Present November–December 1864. NFR. Died 1929.

Pannill, George W. Private, Company C. Born 1847. Enlisted Orange Court House January 15, 1864. Reported present or accounted for on surviving muster rolls through December 31, 1864. NFR. Died 1930. Interred Palmyra Methodist Church Cemetery, Orange County.

Parham, Richard E. Private, Company D. Enlisted Richmond February 19, 1863. NFR.

Parrish, Hillsman. Private, Company B. Enlisted Charlottesville August 25, 1862. Present or accounted for through October 1863. Transferred to

Maryland Line April 1, 1864, but order revoked. Captured Petersburg, West Virginia, July 28, 1864. Took oath in Berlin, Maryland, and was released.

Parrish, John W. Private, Company D. Born 1840. Previously served in Moorman's Virginia Battalion. Enlisted Thirty-Ninth Battalion Orange Court House March 30, 1864. Absent sick in Richmond with typhoid fever August 4, 1864. Absent sick through December 31, 1864. NFR. Died 1874. Interred Locust Level, Louisa County.

Passano, Joshua. Sergeant, Company D. Born 1842. Enlisted Camp Lee January 26, 1863, as private. Promoted to sergeant prior to September 1864. Paroled Appomattox April 9, 1865. Died 1879. Interred Green Mount Cemetery, Baltimore, Maryland.

Patrick, John H. Private, Company B. Previously served in Seventeenth Virginia Infantry. Enlisted Thirty-Ninth Battalion Charlottesville August 25, 1862. Transferred to First Maryland Cavalry April 21, 1864.

Patterson, James L. Private, Company C. Born 1845. Enlisted Orange Court House January 9, 1864. Absent on horse detail October 18–31, 1864. Reported AWOL November 2–December 31, 1864. Paroled Staunton May 22, 1865. Died 1897.

Paul, Thomas H. Private, Company D. Enlisted Danville August 15, 1863. Reported present or accounted for on surviving muster rolls through December 31, 1864. NFR.

Paxson, Thomas M.C. Private, Company A. Born 1833. Previously served in Sixth Virginia Cavalry. Transferred to Thirty-Ninth Battalion February 10, 1864. Detailed to quartermaster's office September–December 1864. Paroled Winchester April 24, 1865. Died 1907. Interred Union Cemetery, Leesburg.

Payne, James A. Private, Company C. Born 1847. Enlisted Lynchburg October 20, 1862. Absent sick Charlottesville August 11, 1863. Released October 5, 1863. Present September–December 1864. Paroled Appomattox Court House April 9, 1865. Died 1934. Interred Riverview Cemetery, Charlottesville.

*Payne, John A. Private, Company A. Born 1831. Previously served in Thirteenth Virginia Infantry. Also served in Forty-Third Battalion Virginia Cavalry.

*Payne, Thomas N. Private, Company E. Enlisted Danville August 15, 1863. NFR.

Peers, William J. Private, Company D. Born 1845. Enlisted Camp Lee February 18, 1863. Absent sick in Richmond October 21–November 1, 1864, with "Ind. Ulcer right leg." Present November–December 1864. Paroled Columbia May 3, 1865.

*Pennill, George W. Private, Company C. Born 1833. Died 1915.

Perkins, Frederick W. Private, Company D. Enlisted Orange Court House March 30, 1864. Reported absent sick September–December 1864. NFR.

Perkins, Joseph. Private, Company B. Born 1839. Enlisted Orange Court House August 18, 1862. Captured near Gettysburg July 1, 1863; however, does not appear in Federal records. NFR. Died 1897. Interred St. Paul's Episcopal Cemetery, Ivy.

Perkins, Richard E. Private, Company D. 1845. Enlisted Camp Lee February 18, 1863. Present or accounted for on surviving muster roll sheets until November–December 1864, when absent on horse detail. Paroled Louisa Court House May 15, 1865.

Perrow, Willis L. Private, Company C. Born 1845. Enlisted Orange Court House January 3, 1864. Present or accounted for through December 1864. Paroled Appomattox Court House April 9, 1865. Died 1895. Interred Presbyterian Cemetery, Lynchburg.

Perry, Artemus H. Private, Company B. Born 1846. Previously served in Sixteenth Virginia Infantry and Manchester Light Artillery. Enlisted Thirty-Ninth Battalion Hamilton's Crossing April 14, 1863. Present through February 1864. Paroled Manchester April 25, 1865.

Persons, Robert T. Private, Company C. Enlisted Macon, Georgia, March 25, 1864. Present through December 1864. Paroled at Appomattox Court House April 9, 1865.

Peterson, William H. Sergeant, Company C. Enlisted Staunton January 5, 1863, as sergeant. Absent sick in Charlottesville May 22, 1864, with "Laryngitis." Transferred to Lynchburg April 26, 1864. Reported absent sick through December 31, 1864. NFR.

Pettigrew, Albert H. First Lieutenant, Company C. Born 1841. Enlisted Lynchburg August 10, 1862, as private. Elected first lieutenant March 9, 1863. Court-martialed March 7, 1864, for violating army regulations. Released from Lynchburg hospital May 31, 1864. Apparently absent sick October 7, 1864–December 31, 1864. NFR. Died 1891. Interred Spring Hill Cemetery, Lynchburg.

Pettis, Thomas. Private, Company D. Enlisted Orange Court House June 1, 1863. Present or accounted for through December 1864. NFR.

Phelps, Lewis A. Private, Company B. Enlisted Orange Court House August 18, 1862. Reported captured October 1862. Present November 1862–February 1863. Discharged April 11, 1863, after being elected to the Virginia House of Delegates.

Pifer, Augustus P. Captain, Company A. Born 1840. Previously served in Third Virginia Infantry and Tenth Virginia Infantry. Elected captain Thirty-Ninth Battalion October 11, 1862. Present on surviving muster roll sheets until absent sick in Richmond September 1–14, 1864, with "debilitas." Reported commanding battalion October 22–31, 1864. Absent on detail January 26, 1865. Relieved from duty March 17, 1865. NFR. Died 1907. Interred Rosemont Cemetery, Newberry, South Carolina.

Pifer, George A. Private, Company A. Born 1843. Enlisted Orange Court House January 3, 1864. Reported present or accounted for on surviving muster rolls. Paroled at Appomattox Court House April 9, 1865. Died 1927. Interred Thornrose Cemetery, Staunton.

Pifer, George W. Private, Company A. Born 1833. Enlisted Orange Court House January 1, 1863. Absent on leave January 4, 1863. Absent sick September–December 1864. Paroled Winchester April 22, 1865. Died 1917. Interred Gravel Springs Cemetery, Frederick County.

*Pifer, Randolph L. Private, Company A. Born 1837. Died 1920. Interred Greenhill Cemetery, Stephens City.

Potter, J.G. Private, Company D. Enlisted Danville May 15, 1863. Died prior to June 1, 1863.

Powers, George W. Private, Company B. Place and date of enlistment unknown. Reported AWOL October 1862.

Preston, Charles J. Private, Company C. Born 1834. Previously served in Fifth Virginia Cavalry. Transferred to Thirty-Ninth Battalion March 1, 1865. Paroled Appomattox Court House April 9, 1865. Died 1894. Interred East Hill Cemetery, Salem.

Preston, Isaac M. Private, Company C. Enlisted Lynchburg January 12, 1863. Present on surviving muster rolls until reported absent sick May–August 1863. Reported present August–December 1864. NFR.

Price, Oliver D. Second Lieutenant, Company B. Born 1833. Previously served in Second Texas Cavalry. Assigned to Thirty-Ninth Battalion July 19, 1863. Absent sick in Richmond August 27–September 5, 1863, with chronic diarrhea. Present or accounted for until absent sick June 30, 1864, in Richmond with chronic diarrhea and spinal irritation. Transferred to Farmville. Furloughed October 26, 1864. Absent sick October 10, 1864, Richmond, with dysentery. Furloughed October 26, 1864. Absent sick Gordonsville December 7, 1864, and Lynchburg January 14–26, 1865. Paroled Burkesville Junction April 14–17, 1865.

Price, Richard J.L. Private, Company B. Enlisted Stone Bridge November 6, 1862. Present through October 31, 1863. Paroled Verdiersville June 3, 1865.

Puryear, William H. Private, Company D. Enlisted Danville May 20, 1863. Present or accounted for through February 22, 1864. Reported AWOL July 10, 1864, through December 31, 1864; however, issued clothing October 20, 1864. NFR.

Ramsey, Alexander J. Private, Company C. Born 1843. Previously served in Fifty-Seventh Virginia Infantry. Enlisted Thirty-Ninth Battalion Lynchburg November 20, 1862. Absent sick in Richmond February 26, 1863. Reported AWOL March–April 1863. Wounded in action, fractured jaw, and in a Richmond hospital May 26, 1863. Furloughed June 11, 1863. Detailed battalion teamster April 20, 1864. Absent sick in Richmond June 8, 1864, with sunstroke. Transferred to Lynchburg July 9, 1864. Furloughed August 24, 1864. Absent sick through December 31, 1864. NFR.

Randolph, William F. Captain, Company B. Born 1831. Previously served in Sixth Virginia Cavalry. Elected captain Thirty-Ninth Battalion August 18, 1862. Present or accounted for until captured in Fauquier County, September 1863; however, not in Federal prisoner records. Relieved from duty February 24, 1864. NFR. Died 1914. Interred Warrenton Cemetery, Warrenton.

Rative, John M. Private, Company C. Born 1838. Enlisted Orange Court House August 18, 1862. Present November 1862–October 1863. NFR until paroled at Edward's Ferry April 29, 1865. Died 1894, West Virginia.

*Rawlings, John B. Private, Company A. Place and date of enlistment unknown. Paroled at Appomattox Court House April 9, 1865. Died 1925. Interred Thornrose Cemetery, Staunton.

Rawlings, Walter M. Private, Company B. Born 1838. Possibly served in a Missouri regiment prior to enlisting in Thirty-Ninth Battalion Charlottesville August 18, 1862 as corporal. Absent sick in Richmond October 18, 1862. Transferred to Farmville November 3, 1862. Present February 1863. Reduced to ranks prior to March 1863. Absent sick Richmond April 6–8, 1864. Paroled Farmville April 11–21, 1865. Died 1897. Interred Holy Trinity Episcopal Church Cemetery, Perquimans County, North Carolina.

Ray, William H. Private, Company A. Enlisted Orange Court House January 7, 1864. Present September–December 1864. Captured Cedar Creek March 7, 1865. Sent to Fort McHenry. Released May 1, 1865.

Read, George. Private, Company D. Born 1844. Previously served in Twentieth Virginia Infantry. Enlisted Thirty-Ninth Battalion Camp Lee February 18, 1863. NFR.

Redmond, George T. Second Lieutenant, Company B. Born 1836. Previously served in First Maryland Infantry. Elected second lieutenant Thirty-Ninth Battalion August 18, 1862. Resigned October 21, 1862. Died 1864, Florida.

Reeves, George C. Private, Company A. Born 1842. Enlisted Winchester October 11, 1862. Reported present or accounted for on surviving muster rolls. Paroled Fairfax Court House April 28, 1865. Died 1924. Interred Oakdale Baptist Church, Prince William County.

Reeves, Lycurgus W. Private, Company D. Born 1845. Enlisted Prince William County July 6, 1863. Reported present or accounted for on surviving muster rolls. Paroled Fairfax Court House May 2, 1865. Died 1870. Interred Prince William County.

Renner, James A. Private, Company A. Enlisted Winchester November 8, 1862. Present on surviving muster rolls through June 1863. Reported AWOL July 17, 1863. Dropped as deserter.

Rice, William D. Private, Company D. Enlisted Orange Court House March 24, 1864. Absent sick, acute dysentery, Richmond, May 29, 1864. Transferred to Farmville. Present September–December 1864. Paroled Appomattox Court House April 9, 1865. Died 1924. Interred Rice and Tate Family Cemetery, Hanover County.

Richards, John. Private, Company B. Born 1844. Enlisted Orange Court House August 12, 1862. Captured Martinsburg September 14, 1864. Sent to Point Lookout, Maryland. Exchanged November 15, 1864. In a Richmond hospital November 28, 1864. Furloughed November 29, 1864. Paroled May 12, 1865.

Richardson, John H. Major, Field and Staff. Born 1828. Previously served as colonel, Forty-Sixth Virginia Infantry. Apparently resigned. Appointed major Thirty-Ninth Battalion September 24, 1862. Wounded in action at Gettysburg July 1863. Present or accounted for through February 1865. NFR. Died 1900. Interred Hollywood Cemetery, Richmond.

Richardson, Thomas L. Private, Company D. Born 1842. Enlisted Danville July 20, 1863. Present or accounted for through September 1, 1863. NFR. Died 1904. Interred Powhatan County.

Rickard, James A. Private, Company C. Born 1844. Enlisted Luray January 9, 1863. Reported present or accounted for on surviving muster rolls. NFR. Died 1911. Interred Rickard Smith Family Graveyard, Page County.

Ridgley, Randolph. Private, Company B. Born 1844. Enlisted Stone Bridge November 1863. Present through October 31, 1862. NFR. Died 1918. Interred Summerville Cemetery, Richmond County, Georgia.

Riley, James W. Private, Company A. Born 1832. Enlisted Winchester October 11, 1862. Captured November 8, 1862. Sent to Old Capitol Prison. Exchanged November 18, 1862. Reported present or accounted for on surviving muster rolls. Paroled Winchester May 2, 1865. Interred Manassas.

Ritter, Walker. Private, Company A. Born 1836. Enlisted Winchester October 11, 1862. Deserted Winchester November 18, 1862. Died 1912. Interred Woodbine Cemetery, Harrisonburg.

Robert, John F. Private, Company C. Enlisted Lynchburg January 15, 1863. Captured Gettysburg July 6, 1863. Admitted to hospital in Frederick, Maryland, with debility July 9, 1863. Transferred to Fort McHenry, then Fort Delaware, July 18, 1863. NFR.

Robinson, C.C. Private, company unknown. Place and date of enlistment unknown. Admitted to a Farmville hospital September 4, 1864. Furloughed September 6, 1864. NFR.

Robinson, David S. Private, Company C. Born 1834. Enlisted Winchester October 11, 1862. Detailed as teamster July–October 1863. Absent sick Richmond with "chronic diarrhoea" June 13–August 3, 1864. Absent sick with dysentery in Richmond September 16–28, 1864. Paroled Appomattox Court House April 9, 1865. Died 1908. Interred Rollins Cemetery, Prince William County.

Robinson, Henry D. Private, Company D. Born 1830. Enlisted Prince William County July 6, 1863. Paroled April 22, 1865. Died 1893. Interred Oak Dale Baptist Church, Cemetery, Prince William County.

Robinson, Robert E. Private, Company D. Previously served in Sixth Virginia Cavalry. Enlisted Thirty-Ninth Battalion Petersburg November 2, 1864. Present through December 31, 1864. Paroled Richmond May 15, 1865.

Rock, Thomas. Private, Company B. Previously served in Thirty-Seventh Virginia Cavalry. Enlisted Thirty-Ninth Battalion Orange Court House August 18, 1862. Wounded and captured September 1, 1862. Returned to Thirty-Ninth Battalion prior to January 1863. Reported AWOL June 15, 1863; however, died of wounds received at Boonesboro, Maryland, July 1863. Possibly interred Thornrose Cemetery, Staunton.

Rodes, John W. Corporal, Company C. Born 1837. Previously served in Seventh Virginia Cavalry. Enlisted Thirty-Ninth Battalion Lynchburg October 1, 1862, as private. Promoted to corporal prior to March 1863. Reported absent on leave October 27–December 31, 1864. NFR. Died 1893. Interred Mount Moriah Methodist Church Cemetery, Albemarle County.

Rodes, Thomas L. Private, Company C. Born 1829. Enlisted Orange County January 21, 1864. Absent sick in Richmond with "Remit fever" September 6–October 20, 1864. Present November 1864. Absent horse detail December 24–31, 1864. NFR. Died 1902. Interred Mount Moriah Methodist Church Cemetery, Albemarle County.

Rollins, Austin. Private, Company A. Born 1836. Enlisted Winchester October 11, 1864. Reported present or accounted for on surviving muster rolls. Paroled Fairfax Court House May 28, 1865. Died 1899. Interred Rollins Cemetery, Prince William County.

Rollins, John W. Private, Company A. Born 1838. Enlisted Winchester October 11, 1862. Reported present or accounted for on surviving muster rolls. Paroled Appomattox Court House April 9, 1865. Died 1921. Interred Rollins Cemetery, Prince William County.

Rothgeb, Abram J. Private, Company C. Born 1843. Previously served in Dixie Artillery and Cayce's Virginia Artillery. Transferred Thirty-Ninth Battalion January 21, 1863. Present or accounted for until through December 31, 1864. Court-martialed on unknown date. NFR. Died 1882. Interred Keyser Cemetery, Page County.

Rothgeb, John W. Private, Company C. Born 1841. Previously served in Dixie Artillery and Cayce's Virginia Artillery. Transferred Thirty-Ninth Battalion January 21, 1863. Reported present or accounted for on surviving muster rolls through December 1864. NFR. Died 1928.

Ruffner, Philip. Corporal, Company C. Born 1832. Enlisted Luray January 1, 1863. Present or accounted for through March 1863. NFR. Died 1909. Interred Ruffner Cemetery, Page County.

Russell, George B. Private, Company A. Enlisted Winchester October 11, 1862. Reported present or accounted for on surviving muster rolls through December 1864. Absent wounded, right foot, Richmond February 10– March 5, 1865. NFR.

Rutledge, John R. Private, Company C. Enlisted Lynchburg November 15, 1862. Detailed to quartermaster's shop April–August 1863. NFR.

***Sale, William D.** Private, Company B. Born 1848. Died 1916. Interred Graham Cemetery, Orange County.

Sandridge, Charles D. Private, Company C. Born 1843. Enlisted Orange Court House January 15, 1864. Detailed Medical Department January 15– December 31, 1864. Paroled Appomattox Court House April 9, 1865. Died 1925. Interred Wesley Chapel Methodist Church, Albemarle County.

Scott, Charles. Private, Company D. Born 1842. Enlisted Camp Lee February 18, 1863. Present June 1–September 1, 1863. NFR.

Seay, Silas M. Private, company unknown. Born 1842. Previously served in Eighth Missouri Cavalry and Goochland Artillery. Place and date of enlistment unknown. Paroled Columbia May 8, 1865. Died 1926. Interred Lyles Baptist Church Cemetery, Fluvanna County.

*Shacklett, J. Private, Company A.

Shacklett, Richard G. Private, Company A. Born 1839. Enlisted December 22, 1863. Detailed to quartermaster's department Columbia, South Carolina, September 30, 1864. Paroled Winchester April 21, 1865. Died 1918. Interred Riverview Cemetery, Strasburg.

Shaver, William H. Private, Company A. Enlisted Winchester October 11, 1862. Absent sick with "Icterus" in Richmond November 22, 1864–January 6, 1865. NFR.

Shaw, John W. Private, Company D. Born 1840. Previously served in Thirteenth Virginia Infantry. Enlisted Thirty-Ninth Battalion, Orange Court House May 28, 1863. Reported present September–December 1864. NFR.

Shelton, George W. Sergeant, Company C. Born 1840. Previously served in Eleventh Virginia Infantry. Enlisted Thirty-Ninth Battalion Lynchburg October 10, 1862. Served as quartermaster sergeant May 1–July 9, 1864. Reduced to the ranks prior to September 1864. Present through December 1864. NFR. Died 1924. Interred Spring Hill Cemetery, Lynchburg.

Shisler, John R. Private, Company C. Born 1827. Previously served in Fifty-Sixth Virginia Infantry. Enlisted Thirty-Ninth Battalion Richmond February 19, 1863. Present or accounted for on surviving muster rolls. Paroled Appomattox Court April 9, 1865.

*Shorter, C.C. Private, Company C. Place and date of enlistment unknown. Place and date of capture unknown. Sent to Camp Morton, Indiana. Died March 22, 1865. Interred Greenlawn Cemetery, Indianapolis, Indiana.

Simpson, George A. Private, Company A. Born 1830. Previously served in Twelfth Virginia Cavalry. Enlisted Thirty-Ninth Battalion Winchester October 11, 1862. Present or accounted for on surviving muster rolls through September 1864. Paroled Fairfax Court House April 26, 1864. Died 1919. Interred Gainesville Methodist Church Cemetery, Prince William County.

Sinnott, James B. First Sergeant, Company B. Born 1842. Previously served in First Louisiana Infantry. Enlisted Thirty-Ninth Battalion Orange Court House August 18, 1862 as sergeant. Promoted to first sergeant prior to October 31, 1863. Present through March 1864. Paroled Winchester. Died 1917. Interred Metairie Cemetery, New Orleans, Louisiana.

Sisk, Charles W. Private, Company D. Born 1823. Previously served in Seventh Virginia Infantry. Enlisted Thirty-Ninth Battalion Rappahannock County June 21, 1863. Reported AWOL November–December 1864. NFR.

Sisk, J.T. Private, Company D. Enlisted Middleburg June 20, 1863. Present or not stated through June 30, 1863. NFR.

Skidmore, John D. Private, Company D. Previously served in unknown Confederate regiment. Enlisted Thirty-Ninth Battalion Orange Court House July 21, 1863. Captured Falls Church August 6, 1864. Sent to Old Capitol Prison, transferred to Elmira. Exchanged March 21, 1865. Absent sick with debility in Charlottesville March 26–27, 1864. Absent sick with "Febris Verrietbilosa" in Gordonsville March 27, 1865. NFR.

Skidmore, Thomas S. Private, Company D. Previously served in Forty-Seventh Virginia Infantry and Thirtieth Virginia Infantry. Enlisted Thirty-Ninth Battalion July 6, 1863. NFR.

Slaughter, Joseph M. Private, Company C. Previously served in Twenty-Eighth Virginia Infantry. Enlisted Thirty-Ninth Battalion Lynchburg October 15, 1862. Present or not stated through December 1864. Paroled at Appomattox Court House April 9, 1865.

*Slaughter, Samuel. Private, Company C.

Sloat, Alexander T. Private, Company A. Born 1831. Enlisted October 11, 1862. Present as bugler January–August 1863. Absent sick, "Remit fever," in Richmond October 21–November 1, 1864. Present through December 1864. NFR. Died 1890. Interred Mount Hebron Cemetery, Winchester.

Sloat, Charles D. Private, Company A. Born 1832. Enlisted Winchester October 11, 1862. Wounded in action Spotsylvania Court House May 31, 1864. Absent detailed with quartermaster's department September–

December 1864. Paroled Appomattox Court House April 9, 1865. Died 1919. Interred Mount Hebron Cemetery, Winchester.

*Sloat, Charles W. Private, Company A.

Sloat, Thomas E. Private, Company A. Born 1833. Enlisted Winchester October 11, 1862. Present through August 1863. NFR. Died 1900. Interred Mount Hebron Cemetery, Winchester.

*Smallwood, Abner. Private, Company A.

Smallwood, James W. Private, Company A. Enlisted Winchester October 11, 1862. Detailed as wagoner. Reported AWOL June 22, 1863. Dropped as a deserter.

Smallwood, Robert A. Private, Company D. Enlisted Orange Court House September 8, 1863. Deserted July 25, 1863.

Smith, F.S. Private, Company D. Place and date of enlistment unknown. Present January 26–April 13, 1863. NFR.

Smith, George W. Private, Company B. Born 1796. Enlisted Orange Court House August 18, 1862. Wounded Chancellorsville May 2, 1863 ("head implical-bone with Erysipelas & Gangrene"). Absent wounded through June 30, 1863. Furloughed June 30, 1863. Present March 1864. NFR. Died 1885. Interred Maplewood Cemetery, Orange County.

*Smith, John R. Private, Company A.

*Smith, Joshua S. Private, Company A. Born 1838. Died 1907. Interred Goose Creek Burying Ground, Loudon County.

Smith, Lloyd T. Sergeant, Company B. Born 1845. Enlisted Orange Court House August 18, 1862. Present or accounted for through April 1863. Absent sick Charlottesville with "typhoid fever" December 24, 1863–January 19, 1864. Paroled Fairfax Court House April 22, 1865. Died 1904. Interred Smith Cemetery, Northumberland County.

Smith, Marshal G. Private, Company D. Born 1827. Enlisted Camp Lee February 18, 1863. NFR.

Smith, Phillip. Private, Company B. Enlisted Salem September 15, 1862. Present or accounted for through April 1863. Promoted to sergeant May 1, 1863. Reported under arrest October 28–31, 1863, and reduced in ranks to private. Discharged February 19, 1864.

*Smith, Robert M. Private, Company B. Born 1845. Died 1932. Interred Thornrose Cemetery, Staunton.

Smith, T.W. Private, Company A. Place and date of enlistment unknown. Paroled Winchester April 27, 1865.

Smith, Thomas R. Private, Company B. Enlisted Orange Court House August 18, 1862. Court-martialed February 23, 1865. NFR. Manassas Cemetery, Manassas.

Snook, Jerome A. Private, Company A. Enlisted Gettysburg, Pennsylvania, July 3, 1863. Transferred to First Maryland Cavalry December 27, 1863. Died 1881. Interred Mount Olivet Cemetery, Frederick, Maryland.

Speck, John C. Private, Company C. Born 1845. Enlisted Orange Court House November 1, 1863. Died of disease June 30, 1864. Interred Hebron Presbyterian Church Cemetery, Augusta County.

Spicer, Walker W. Private, Company D. Born 1846. Enlisted Orange Court House March 19, 1864. Present September–December 1864. NFR. Died 1932. Interred Walker's Methodist Church Cemetery, Madison County.

Spillman, John H. Private, Company C. Born 1843. Enlisted Richmond February 18, 1863. Transferred Fifty-Second Virginia Infantry in exchange for William Kerr. Killed July 3, 1863, Gettysburg, Pennsylvania.

Stack, John P. Private, Company D. Place and date of enlistment unknown. Deserted Williamsburg February 24, 1864.

St. Clair, Charles W. Private, Company D. Enlisted Middleburg May 10, 1863. Possibly transferred to Thirty-Fifth Virginia Cavalry. Died of wounds December 16, 1864. Interred Confederate Cemetery, Charlottesville.

Steers, William. Private, Company B. Born 1841. Previously served in Twenty-Seventh Virginia Infantry. Transferred to Thirty-Ninth Battalion March 15, 1863. Present or accounted for on surviving muster rolls through December 31, 1864. NFR. Died 1927. Interred Yell Cemetery, Benton County, Arkansas.

Stephens, Eugene A.M. Sergeant, Company D. Enlisted Camp Lee March 23, 1862. Promoted corporal prior to April 1864. Absent sick in Richmond April 16–17, 1864. Promoted to sergeant December 1, 1864. Present through December 31, 1864. Paroled Louisa Court House May 15, 1865.

Stickle, Henry C. Private, Company A. Born 1839. Enlisted Winchester October 11, 1862. Enlisted Eleventh Virginia Cavalry without permission November 6, 1862. Died 1919. Interred Berryville Cemetery, Clarke County.

Stine, William. Private, Company B. Enlisted September 1, 1862. Transferred to Twenty-Seventh Virginia Infantry December 23, 1862.

Stoneberger, Andrew G. Private, Company C. Born 1845. Enlisted Luray February 1, 1863. Court-martialed for theft January 27, 1863. Reported present September–December 1864. NFR. Died 1901. Interred Lucas-Stoneberger Cemetery, Page County.

Stoneberger, George. Private, Company C. Enlisted Luray February 10, 1863. Court-martialed for theft January 27, 1864, and fined five months' pay. Absent sick in a Richmond hospital with rheumatism September 15, 1864. Furloughed September 20, 1864. Absent sick through December 31, 1864. NFR.

Stoneberger, Siram/Siron. Private, Company C. Enlisted Luray February 1, 1863. Absent on leave March–September 1863. Court-martialed for theft January 27, 1863. Present September–December 1864. Captured Petersburg April 3, 1865. Sent to Hart's Island, New York. Released June 6, 1865.

Stribling, John W. Sergeant, Company B. Born 1824. Previously served in unknown Confederate regiment. Enlisted Thirty-Ninth Battalion Orange Court House June 18, 1862. Promoted to sergeant February 28, 1863. Present or accounted for through October 1863. Died February 17, 1864. Interred Thornrose Cemetery, Staunton.

Stringfellow, R.R. Private, Company B. Born 1846. Previously served in Hanover Artillery. Enlisted Thirty-Ninth Battalion 1864. Wounded, left foot, September 1, 1864. Detailed for clerical duty in a Danville hospital December 31, 1864. Furloughed January 24, 1865. Reported in a Richmond hospital April 1, 1865. Paroled Ashland April 24, 1865.

Stringfellow, Robert S. First Sergeant, Company B. Born 1831. Enlisted Stone Bridge November 6, 1862. Captured Loudoun County September 1863; however, not reported in Federal records. Wounded May 2, 1864, in left thigh and sent to Richmond, then transferred to Charlottesville. Furloughed June 21, 1864. Promoted to first sergeant prior to September 1864. Present through September 1864. NFR. Died 1882. Interred Ivy Hill Cemetery, Alexandria.

Strosnider, Simon W. Private, Company A. Born 1834. Enlisted Winchester October 11, 1862. Deserted November 18, 1862. Died 1912. Interred Riverview Cemetery, Strasburg.

Sullivan, Jerry C. Private, Company B. Born 1831. Previously served in Staunton Artillery. Place and date of enlistment in Thirty-Ninth Battalion unknown. Reported AWOL November 27, 1862. Later served in Nineteenth Virginia Infantry.

Sullivan, Michael. Private, Company C. Born 1843. Previously served in Fifteenth Virginia Infantry. Enlisted Thirty-Ninth Battalion Richmond March 2, 1863. Reported AWOL through April 30, 1863. Dropped as a deserter. Died 1905. Interred Mount Cavalry Cemetery, Richmond.

Sutton, Frank T. Private, Company C. Born 1846. Previously served in Moorman's Virginia Battery. Transferred on unknown date to Thirty-Ninth Battalion. NFR. Died 1917. Interred Hollywood Cemetery, Richmond.

Swan, James A. Private, Company A. Born 1839. Enlisted Orange Court House September 23, 1863. Detailed as blacksmith November 1863–December 1864. Paroled Appomattox Court House April 9, 1865. Died 1925. Interred Fairview Cemetery, Culpeper County.

Swartz, Charles. Private, Company A. Born 1832. Previously served in Second Virginia Infantry. Enlisted Thirty-Ninth Battalion Winchester October 11, 1862. Detailed as battalion teamster November 1863–December 1864. Paroled Appomattox Court House April 9, 1865. Died 1887. Interred Green Hill Cemetery, Clarke County.

Swift, Charles W. Private, Company C. Enlisted Orange Court House February 1, 1864. Absent sick with rheumatism in Richmond June 13–27, 1864. Present September–December 1864. Paroled Ashland May 2, 1865.

Talby, William. Private, Company B. Enlisted Orange Court House August 18, 1862. Reported AWOL December 25, 1862–January 1863. Reported absent on detail April 28, 1863. NFR.

Taliaferro, Catlett C.C. Private, Company B. Born 1846. Previously served Ninth Virginia Cavalry. Enlisted Thirty-Ninth Battalion Orange Court House January 6, 1864. Absent sick with boils in Richmond May 29–April 7, 1864. Absent sick with boils and acute dysentery in Farmville November 8, 1864. Returned January 5, 1865. Paroled Appomattox Court House April 9, 1865. Died 1916. Interred College Church Cemetery, Prince Edward County.

Taliaferro, Fitzhugh. Private, Company C. Born 1827. Previously served in Fourth Virginia Cavalry. Enlisted Thirty-Ninth Battalion Orange Court House January 18, 1864. Present June–December 1864. Paroled Appomattox Court House April 9, 1865. Died 1923. Interred Taliaferro Cemetery, Madison County.

Taliaferro, Horace G. Private, Company C. Born 1846. Previously served in Fredericksburg Artillery. Enlisted Thirty-Ninth Battalion January 1, 1864. Absent sick with bronchitis January 24, 1864. Absent sick with "debilitas" in Farmville March 22–April 27, 1864. Absent sick with boils and debility in Farmville July 16–28, 1864. Absent sick with "Fev. Remit." September 13–October 10, 1864. Furloughed October 11, 1864. Absent sick with rheumatism in Farmville November 25–January 18, 1865. Paroled Farmville November 25–January 18, 1865. Died 1897. Interred Westview Cemetery, Prince Edward County.

Tate, Vincent S. Private, Company D. Born 1832. Enlisted Danville May 22, 1863. Present or accounted for through October 1864. Absent on horse detail November–December 1864. NFR. Died 1908. Interred Hopewell Methodist Church Cemetery, Pittsylvania County.

Tatum, Robert F. Private, Company D. Enlisted Orange Court House March 19, 1864. Present September–December 1864. NFR.

Taylor, George W. Private, Company A. Born 1835. Enlisted Winchester October 11, 1862. Detailed company wagoner June 15–August 31, 1863. Detailed as battalion teamster September–December 1864. Paroled Appomattox Court House April 9, 1865. Died 1912. Frederick County.

Taylor, Holbrook. Private, Company D. Enlisted Camp Lee December 20, 1862. Captured and sent to Old Capitol prison. Took oath and was released March 22, 1864.

Taylor, Richard S. Private, Company D. Enlisted Charlottesville May 10, 1863. Present through December 31, 1864, on surviving muster rolls. Paroled Burkesville April 24, 1865.

Taylor, William H. Private, Company C. Born 1838. Enlisted Luray May 1, 1863. Court-martialed for desertion January 27, 1864. Present through December 31, 1864. NFR.

Temple, Eustace. Private, Company A. Born 1841. Enlisted Orange Court House January 13, 1864. Present September–December 1864. NFR. Died 1909, Orange County.

Temple, Robert G. First Lieutenant, Company D. Born 1840. Previously served in Twentieth Virginia Infantry. Elected first lieutenant Thirty-Ninth Battalion January 26, 1864. Died of typhoid fever in Orange Court House March 9, 1864. Interred Ampthill Cemetery, Chesterfield County.

Terrill, John H. Private, Company C. Enlisted Orange Court House January 10, 1864. Present September–December 1864. NFR.

Terrill, Thomas. Private, Company A. Enlisted Orange Court House January 13, 1864. Present September–December 1864. NFR.

*Terrill, William E.T. Private, Company A. Born 1843. Died 1914. Interred Graham Cemetery, Orange County.

Thaxton, William C. Private, Company B. Place and date of enlistment unknown. Paroled Appomattox Court House April 9, 1865.

Thomas, Henry A. Private, Company D. Enlisted Richmond February 12, 1863. Present or accounted for on surviving muster rolls through December 1864. NFR. Died 1910. Interred Woodberry Cemetery, Orange County.

Thomas, Joshua. Private, Company D. Born 1841. Previously served in Seventeenth Virginia Infantry. Detailed as clerk to Army of Northern Virginia headquarters 1862–1864. Transferred to Thirty-Ninth Battalion March 2, 1864. Reported as detailed to Army of Northern Virginia headquarters through December 1864. Paroled at Appomattox Court House April 9, 1865. Died 1920. Interred St. Paul's Cemetery, Alexandria.

Thompson, A. Private, Company C. Place and date of enlistment unknown. Reported absent sick in Richmond with "Int fever Quot" September 16–October 20, 1864. NFR.

Thompson, James S. Private, Company D. Enlisted Danville April 10, 1863. Present or accounted for through September 1, 1863. Transferred to Richmond Fayette Artillery September 12, 1864.

Thompson, Nicholas. Private, Company C. Enlisted Lynchburg January 1, 1863. Present or accounted for through December 1864. NFR.

Thompson, Thomas W. Lieutenant, Company B. Previously served in Nineteenth Virginia Infantry and Fifty-Seventh Virginia Infantry. Place and date of enlistment in Thirty-Ninth Battalion unknown. Paroled Appomattox Court House April 9, 1865. Interred Thompson Cemetery, Albemarle County.

Thurston, John C. Private, Company C. Born 1844. Enlisted Columbia August 15, 1863. Present or accounted for through September 1, 1863. NFR. Died 1911. Interred Riverview Cemetery, Charlottesville.

Tillman, John T. Private, Company B. Enlisted January 3, 1865. NFR. Died 1905. Interred Hillsborough Baptist Church Cemetery, Albemarle County.

Tillman, Thomas W. Private, Company D. Enlisted Charlottesville August 6, 1863. Absent sick Charlottesville with lumbago October 10–November 3, 1863. Wounded in left hand, Shady Grove June 11, 1864. Absent sick Richmond with acute dysentery through June 27, 1864. Absent sick Charlottesville July 28, 1864–March 3, 1865. "Left when Sheridan came." NFR.

Timberlake, Joseph. Private, Company D. Born 1842. Enlisted Petersburg September 23, 1864. Present through December 1864. NFR. Died 1921. Interred Riverview Cemetery, Strasburg.

Toney, George M. Private, Company D. Born 1844. Previously served in Twenty-First Virginia Infantry. Enlisted Thirty-Ninth Battalion Richmond February 18, 1863. Reported as a deserter July 1, 1864, but reportedly was in hospital. Transferred to Twenty-Fifth Battalion Virginia Infantry.

Tongue, Henry M. Corporal, Company B. Born 1842. Enlisted Richmond August 29, 1862. Promoted to corporal prior to October 6, 1864, when he was captured at Rapidan Station. Sent to Point Lookout. Exchanged on unknown date. Paroled Ashland April 26, 1865. Died 1925. Interred Anne's Episcopal Church Cemetery, Annapolis, Maryland.

*Towson, Henry C. Private, company unknown.

*Towson, John W. Private, company unknown. Born 1839. Previously served in Fourth Virginia Cavalry. Died 1920. Interred Shelbina City Cemetery, Shelbina, Missouri.

Trussell, Samuel M. Private, Company A. Enlisted Winchester October 11, 1862. Apparently transferred to Eleventh Virginia Cavalry August 31, 1863.

Tucker, Archer. Private, Company D. Born 1840. Enlisted Camp Lee February 18, 1863. NFR.

Tucker, Richard W. Private, Company D. Born 1845. Enlisted Camp Lee February 18, 1863. Present or accounted for on surviving muster rolls through December 1864. Transferred to Thirty-Eighth Virginia Infantry December 12, 1864.

*Turk, B.S. Enlisted June 1864, Augusta County. NFR.

Turk, Hugh F. Sergeant, Company C. Born 1837. Previously served in Fourteenth Virginia Cavalry and First Virginia Cavalry. Enlisted Thirty-Ninth Battalion Staunton December 16, 1862. Promoted to sergeant July 1, 1863. Present through December 1864. Paroled Staunton May 12, 1865. Died 1905. Interred Tinkling Spring Presbyterian Church, Augusta County.

Turner, Franklin. Private, Company C. Previously served in Thirty-Third Virginia Infantry. Enlisted Thirty-Ninth Battalion Luray March 1, 1863. Deserted August 31, 1863. NFR.

Turner, Thomas S. First Lieutenant, Company B. Elected first lieutenant Orange Court House August 18, 1862. Absent on detached service March 22–April 30, 1863. Absent under arrest awaiting court-martial December 26, 1863. Present March 1, 1864, until reported absent sick with "debilitas" in Charlottesville December 18–21, 1864. NFR.

*Turner, W.W. Private, Company B.

Turner, William W. Private, Company C. Enlisted Lynchburg January 15, 1863. Absent sick with debility in Richmond May 19, 1864. Returned August 25, 1864. Present or accounted for August 26–December 1864. Paroled at Appomattox Court House April 9, 1865.

Twyman, Anthony. Private, Company C. Enlisted Orange Court House February 20, 1864. Reported AWOL August 25–October 31, 1864. Present November–December 1864. Paroled Charlottesville May 18, 1865.

Tyler, James M. Private, Company D. Previously served in Parker's Virginia Battery. Enlisted Thirty-Ninth Battalion October 1863. Paroled Appomattox Court House April 9, 1865.

Upshur, Thomas T. Second Lieutenant, Company B. Born 1844. Previously served in Thirty-Ninth Virginia Infantry. Enlisted Thirty-Ninth Battalion Richmond October 29, 1862. Absent sick with "Int fever" in Richmond September 14–October 11, 1863. Present or accounted for through April 1, 1864. Paroled Richmond May 1, 1865. Died 1910. Interred Upshur Cemetery, Northampton County.

Vaughan, Andrew J. Private, Company D. Enlisted Danville May 26, 1863. Present or accounted for on surviving muster rolls through December 1864. NFR.

*Vaughan, Joseph G. Private, company unknown.

Vorous, John A. Private, Company A. Enlisted Winchester October 11, 1862. Present through August 31, 1863. NFR.

Walke, William T. Adjutant, Field and Staff. Born 1838. Previously served in Sixth Virginia Infantry, Fifth Virginia Cavalry and Fifteenth Virginia Cavalry. Appointed adjutant and transferred to Thirty-Ninth Battalion March 30, 1864, or April 15, 1864. Present through November 1864. Absent on leave December 17–31, 1864. Paroled Greensboro, North Carolina., May 1, 1865. Died 1905. Interred Elmwood Cemetery, Norfolk.

Wall, James F. Private, Company D. Born 1847. Enlisted Prince William County, July 6, 1863. Present September–December 1864. Paroled Fairfax Court House May 2, 1865.

Wall, Robert. Private, Company D. Enlisted Greenwich July 6, 1863. NFR.

*Wallace, J.W. Enlisted March 1863, Augusta County, NFR.

Walter, Franklin G. Private, Company A. Born 1837. Enlisted Winchester October 11, 1862. Absent on duty at quartermaster's office through March 31, 1864. Paroled New Market May 20, 1865. Died 1930. Interred Mount Hebron Cemetery, Winchester.

Walton, Edward. Private, Company D. Born 1847. Previously served in Cumberland Reserves. Transferred to Thirty-Ninth Battalion November 1, 1864. Paroled April 26, 1865. Died 1923. Cumberland County.

Walton, Nathaniel W. Sergeant, Company D. Born 1832. Enlisted Camp Lee February 19, 1863. Promoted to sergeant prior to September 1, 1864. Present through December 1864. Paroled Burksville April 26, 1865.

Ward, William S. Sergeant, Company A. Born 1837. Enlisted Winchester October 11, 1862 as sergeant. Absent on detail at Army of Northern Virginia headquarters February 8, 1863–December 1864. Paroled Appomattox April 9, 1865.

Warder, James H. Private, Company A. Enlisted Richmond October 20, 1863. Absent sick Staunton with fever December 30, 1864. Reported AWOL December 20–31, 1864. Deserted March 8, 1865, and took oath in Alexandria March 20, 1865.

Watkins, Thomas A. Private, Company D. Born 1844. Enlisted Halifax County June 1, 1863. Absent sick in Danville with chronic diarrhea July 21–August 21, 1864. Reported AWOL September–December 1864. Paroled May 9, 1865.

Watson, William. Private, Company D. Previously served Second Virginia Infantry. Enlisted Thirty-Ninth Battalion June 15, 1863. Present or accounted for through June 30, 1864. NFR.

Wayts, Samuel. Private, Company B. Place and date of enlistment unknown. Reported AWOL October 1862.

Weaver, Lewis. Private, Company B. Born 1840. Place and date of enlistment unknown. Captured Rapidan Station October 9, 1864. Sent to Point Lookout, Maryland. Released June 8, 1865. Died 1924. Interred Auburn Cemetery, Montgomery County.

Weisher, Michael. Private, Company B. Enlisted Staunton October 29, 1862. Transferred to First Maryland Cavalry March 31, 1864.

Welch, William. Private, Company B. Born 1840. Enlisted Orange Court House August 18, 1862. Absent sick in Richmond with sore throat November 27, 1862–January 11, 1863. Reported absent on leave March 25, 1863. AWOL through October 31, 1863. Dropped as a deserter.

Weller, William H. Private, Company C. Born 1840. Enlisted Staunton August 18, 1862. Reported captured October 1862. Present November 1862–April 1863. Absent sick March–June 1863. Present July–October 1863. Paroled Staunton May 20, 1865. Died 1893. Interred Thornrose Cemetery, Staunton.

*Wheelhouse, J.B. Private, company unknown. Place and date of enlistment unknown. Paroled Greensboro, North Carolina, May 2, 1865.

Whetzel, John M. Private, Company A. Enlisted Winchester November 18, 1862. Present through May 1863. Died of disease May 4, 1863, at Spotsylvania Court House.

White, James. Corporal, Company A. Born 1844. Enlisted October 11, 1862 as corporal. Present or accounted for through December 1864. Paroled Winchester April 22, 1865.

White, Mordecai E. Private, Company A. Born 1811. Enlisted Winchester October 11, 1862. Detailed to quartermaster's department April 12–December 31, 1864. NFR. Died 1905. Interred Frederick.

White, Samuel F. Private, Company C. Born 1838. Enlisted Staunton December 18, 1862. Captured Gettysburg, Pennsylvania, July 2, 1863. Sent to Fort Delaware. Exchanged October 5, 1864. Reported sick in Richmond November 20–21, 1864. Paroled Winchester April 30, 1865.

Whitehurst, William H. Private, Company B. Born 1839. Previously served in Weisinger's company and Sixteenth Virginia Infantry. Enlisted Thirty-Ninth Battalion 1862 without authority. Absent sick November 1, 1862–February 28, 1863. Present March–August 1863. Absent sick with dyspepsia and hepatitis in Richmond December 30, 1863–November 29, 1864. NFR.

Williams, John. Private, Company B. Enlisted Orange Court House August 18, 1862. Absent awaiting trial November 1862–February 1863. Court-martialed March 26, 1863. Present on surviving muster rolls March 1864. NFR.

Williamson, Thomas V. Sergeant, Company D. Born 1826. Enlisted Lynchburg September 1, 1862. Captured May 3, 1863, at Fredericksburg. Sent to Old Capitol Prison. Transferred to Fort Delaware. Exchanged May 23, 1863. Absent sick with rheumatism in Richmond September 20–December 31, 1864. Paroled Winchester May 3, 1864.

Willingham, Jacob H. Private, Company A. Born 1840. Enlisted Winchester October 11, 1862. Absent sick Clarke County November 17–December 31, 1862. Present or accounted for through November 1864. Absent on horse detail December 24–31, 1864. Paroled Appomattox Court House April 9, 1865. Died 1919. Interred Old Chapel Cemetery, Clarke County.

Willingham, John T. Private, Company A. Born 1828. Enlisted Winchester October 11, 1862. Transferred Sixth Virginia Cavalry October 6, 1863.

Wilson, John. Private, Company A. Enlisted October 11, 1862. Reported AWOL October 18, 1862. Dropped as a deserter.

Wilson, Thomas. Private, Company D. Born 1844. Place and date of enlistment unknown. Present or accounted for June 1–September 1, 1863. NFR. Died 1923. Interred Mount Ararat Baptist Church Cemetery, Stafford County.

Wilson, Valerius W. Sergeant, Company B. Born 1839. Previously served in Second Virginia Infantry. Transferred to Thirty-Ninth Battalion April 1, 1862 as sergeant. Absent sick with "Catalepsy" in Charlottesville February 4–28, 1863. Discharged by reason of "Catilipti." Died 1902. Interred Geraldstown Cemetery, Berkeley County, West Virginia.

Winder, Daniel H. Sergeant, Company C. Enlisted Richmond February 1, 1863, as a sergeant. Reduced to the ranks prior to May 1863 when reported AWOL. Dropped as a deserter.

Winsatt, John S. Private, Company D. Born 1848. Previously served in Sixth Virginia Cavalry. Enlisted Thirty-Ninth Battalion Orange Court House July 21, 1863. Reported AWOL June 24, 1864. Reported present September–December 1864. Transferred to Seventeenth Virginia Infantry January 1, 1865.

Winsatt, R. Private, Company D. Enlisted Greenwich July 6, 1863. NFR.

Wise, William H. Private, Company D. Born 1841. Previously served in unknown Confederate regiment. Enlisted Thirty-Ninth Battalion Richmond February 19, 1863. Transferred to Trans-Mississippi in 1864. Died 1909. Interred Greenwood Cemetery, Caddo Parish, Louisiana.

Wisher, Michael. Private, Company B. Enlisted Staunton October 29, 1862. Transferred to Maryland Line March 31, 1864.

Withers, Austin C. Corporal, Company B. Born 1841. Enlisted Richmond August 29, 1862. Promoted to corporal prior to March 1863. Present through February 1864. NFR. Died 1883. Interred Cedar Hill Cemetery, Suffolk.

Wolfe, Robert T. Private, Company D. Born 1844. Enlisted Camp Lee November 28, 1862, as sergeant. Reduced to the ranks prior to 1865. Paroled Greensboro, North Carolina, May 1, 1865. Died 1900. Interred Fredericksburg Cemetery, Fredericksburg.

Womack, L. Sergeant, company unknown. Place and date of enlistment unknown. Absent sick with typhoid fever in Danville October 2, 1862. Furloughed November 22, 1862. NFR.

Wood, Samuel R. Sergeant, Company D. Born 1835. Enlisted Charlottesville May 20, 1863. Promoted to sergeant prior to August 4, 1864. Reported absent sick with debility in Richmond August 4, 1864. Died of typhoid fever August 11, 1864. Interred Spring Garden Cemetery, Fluvanna County.

Woods, James T. Private, Company A. Born 1843. Previously served in Eleventh Virginia Infantry. Transferred to Thirty-Ninth Battalion March 12, 1864. Present September–December 1864. NFR. Died 1911. Interred St. Luke's Episcopal Church Cemetery, Amherst County.

*Yeakley, Martin F. Private, Company A. Born 1835. Died 1909. Interred Mount Hebron Cemetery, Winchester.

*Yeatts, Daniel. Private, Company D.

*Young, James A. Private, Company A.

Zea, Joseph S. Sergeant, Company A. Enlisted Winchester October 11, 1862, as quartermaster sergeant. Promoted to sergeant prior to May 1863. Reported AWOL October 2–December 31, 1864. Paroled at Appomattox Court House April 9, 1865.

Zeaker, W.A. Private, company unknown. Place and date of enlistment unknown. Wounded and captured at Wilderness Tavern May 10, 1864. Transferred to Fredericksburg. NFR.

Notes

Introduction

1. Dowdey, *Lee's Last Campaign*, 26.
2. *Asheville Citizen-Times*, March 3, 1916.

Chapter 1: 1862

3. *Regulations for the Army of the Confederate States*, 51–52, 57.
4. *Confederate Veteran*, vol. 39, July 1931, 248.
5. While the Confederate Conscription Act was passed on April 16, 1862, men were able to volunteer with regiments of their own choosing through late summer of 1862.
6. *Biographical and Historical Memoirs of Mississippi*, 2:12; William F. Randolph, compiled military service record, M324, Roll070, RG109, National Archives.
7. Pfanz, *Letters of Richard S. Ewell*, 222–23; 1860 US Census; Driver and Ruffner, *1st Battalion Virginia Infantry*, 147, 150, 156. Donald Pfanz, in his biography of Richard Ewell, writes that there was some "salty locution between the members of Captain Elijah V. White's Thirty-Fifth Virginia Cavalry Battalion" and Ewell. White's men were serving as Ewell's scouts and couriers. This might have led to the formation of Ewell's Body Guard. Pfanz, *Richard S. Ewell*, 168.
8. Driver and Ruffner, *1st Battalion Virginia Infantry*, 135, 150, 152.

9. *Official Records of the War of the Rebellion Series 1*, 12: part 2, 176. [Hereafter cited as "OR." All entries refer to Series 1 unless otherwise noted.]
10. Myers, *The Comanches*, 95, 97–98.
11. Ibid., 99–100; Jones, *Campbell Brown's Civil War*, 154; Thomas Rook, compiled military service records, M324, Roll 199, Record Group 109, National Archives. [Hereafter cited as "CMSR" unless otherwise noted.]
12. Myers, *The Comanches*, 102; Jones, *Campbell Brown's Civil War*, 158; Ewell, *Virginia Scenes*, 63–64.
13. *Richmond Dispatch*, September 25, 1862; William W. Page, CMSR.
14. Burns, *Curiosities of the Confederate Capital*, 54–64.
15. Keen and Mewborn, *43rd Battalion Virginia Cavalry*, 355; Driver and Ruffner, *1st Battalion Virginia Infantry*, 148; Hewett, *Supplement to the OR*, 70: 211.
16. *Richmond Dispatch*, September 10, 1853; April 2, 1856; February 22, 1858; May 30, 1861; Allardice, *Confederate Colonels*, 323. Hugh W. Fry Jr., major of the Forty-Sixth Virginia infantry, wrote a letter to the secretary of war on May 28, 1862, claiming voting irregularities. Letters received by the Confederate Secretary of War, 1861–1865. M437, Roll68, RG109, National Archives.
17. *Richmond Daily Dispatch*, October 10, 1862.
18. Driver and Ruffner, *1st Battalion Virginia Infantry*, 131, 139, 149; Cartmell, *Shenandoah Valley Pioneers*, 320.
19. Greene, *Stony Mead*, 21.
20. Cartmell, *Shenandoah Valley Pioneers*, 320; Driver and Ruffner. *1st Battalion Virginia Infantry*, 51–52.
21. *Richmond Dispatch*, September 1, 1862; *Daily Dispatch*, November 15, 1862.
22. OR 21: 1039, 1041, 1045.
23. Ibid., 667.
24. *Supplement to the OR*, 70: 208.
25. OR 21: 668.

Chapter 2: 1863

26. John R. Lupton to "Dear Father," January 13, 1862, February 19, 1863, Helena Knight Lupton Collection; *Supplement to the OR*, 70: 208; Anthony Butts, CMSR.
27. Taylor, *General Lee*, 154; Wiley, *Reminiscences of Confederate Service*, 88; *Birmingham Daily Post*, January 1, 1862.

28. John R. Lupton to sister, February 19, 1863, Lupton papers; Thomas G. Lupton to sister, February 19, 1863, Helena Knight Lupton Collection.
29. Albert H. Pettigrew and Samuel B. Brown, CMSR; Driver and Ruffner, *1st Battalion Virginia Cavalry*, 132, 145.
30. Jessup, *Painful News*, 130, 135.
31. John. R. Lupton to "Dear Mother," April 19, 1863, Helena Knight Lupton Collection.
32. Bigelow, *Campaign of Chancellorsville*, 236.
33. Thomas Lupton to "My dear sister," May 21, 1863 Helena Knight Lupton Collection.
34. Randolph, "With Stonewall Jackson at Chancellorsville," 24.
35. Others in Jackson's party included Captain Richard Wilbourn, signal officer; Lieutenant Joseph Morrison, aide-de-camp; Private William Wynn, signal corps; Private William Cunliffe, signal corps; and Private David Kyle, Ninth Virginia Cavalry. Robertson, *Stonewall Jackson*, 726.
36. Randolph, "With Stonewall Jackson at Chancellorsville," 24; *Land We Love* (July 1866), 181; Clark, *Histories of Several Regiments*, 5:99.
37. Randolph, "With Stonewall Jackson at Chancellorsville," 24. There are many sources that state Joshua Johns was a member of the Thirty-Ninth Battalion at the time of the battle of Chancellorsville. However, his compiled service record states he did not join the battalion until December 21, 1863. See Krick, *Smoothbore Volley*, 30. Randolph's account varies greatly from other narratives by the participants. He states he was the only one with Jackson until Hill arrived. However, it was Wilbourn and Wynn who lifted Jackson out of the saddle and placed him on the ground. Furthermore, according to most accounts, it was Wilbourn who sent Wynn to find a surgeon. It is possible that Hill also ordered Randolph to seek a doctor. See Robertson, *Stonewall Jackson*, 731.
38. Randolph writes that it was Jackson's chief of staff, Sandie Pendleton, who ordered him to find Stuart. Randolph, "With Stonewall Jackson at Chancellorsville," 23. A.P. Hill, in his official report, simply writes that Stuart was sent for and not who made the decision. *OR*, 25: 885–886.
39. George Smith, CMSR; *Manassas Journal*, August 27, 1931; Driver and Ruffner, *1st Battalion Virginia Infantry*, 152, 153, 157; Jessup, *Painful News*, 139.
40. Samuel Brown, CMSR; Driver and Ruffner, *1st Battalion Virginia Infantry*, 149; *Evening Messenger*, March 26, 1900.
41. Driver and Ruffner, *1st Battalion Virginia Infantry*, 134, 137.

42. Samuel Brown, CMSR; Jessup, *Painful News*, 141; Swank, *Courier for Lee and Jackson*, 41.

43. Walter, diary, June 22–26, 1863; *Alexander Gazette*, October 9, 1892; Francis Dawson writes that a group of ladies was waiting for Lee as he crossed the Potomac River with a wreath for Lee's horse. The horse balked, and Lee gave the wreath to a courier. Wiley, *Reminiscences of Confederate Service*, 91.

44. The *Alexander Gazette* reported, "Three of General Lee's body-guard were captured to night," July 6, 1863; OR 27, pt 1: 923; *Manassas Journal*, August 27, 1931. E. Porter Alexander writes that a courier captured at Greencastle bore a dispatch from Davis to Lee discussing a demonstration by P.G.T. Beauregard in front of Washington, D.C. Gallagher, ed. *Fighting for the Confederacy*, 247.

45. Walter, diary, July 1, 1863; Smith, *Story of Lee's Headquarters*, 40–41; Maurice, *Aide-de-Camp of Lee*, 233.

46. Hewett, *Supplement to the OR*, 70: 208, 210; *Baltimore Sun*, July 4, 1913; Walter, diary, July 2, 1863; *Times*, November 30, 1900.

47. Walter, diary, July 4–7, 1863.

48. Jones, *Campbell Brown's Civil War*, 226.

49. Walter, diary, July 7, 1863.

50. John R. Lupton to "Dear mother and father," July 9, 1863, Helena Knight Lupton Collection; Jessup, *Painful News*, 148.

51. Walter, diary, July 10, 1863; Hewett, *Supplement to the OR*, 70: 210; OR 27, pt. 3: 994.

52. Walter, diary, 11–17, 1863.

53. Driver and Ruffner, *1st Battalion Virginia Infantry*, 60.

54. Jones, *Campbell Brown's Civil War*, 234, 235; Thomas Lupton to "dear sister," John R. Lupton to "Dear Sister," October 17, 1863, Helena Knight Lupton Collection.

55. Thomas Lupton to "Sister," November 1, 1863, Helena Knight Lupton Collection.

56. *Sentinel*, April 8, 1864; John R. Lupton to "Dear Father," August 23, 1863, Helena Knight Lupton Collection; Jessup, *Painful News*, 153; Thomas Lupton to "Dear Sisters," September 16, 1863, Helena Knight Lupton Collection.

57. Thomas Lupton to "Dear Sisters," September 16, 1863, November 1, 1863, Helena Knight Lupton Collection; Thomas Lupton to "Dear Cousin John," October 23, 1863, Helena Knight Lupton Collection; Jessup, *Painful News*, 158.

58. Tower, *Lee's Adjutant*, 83, 85.

Chapter 3: 1864

59. Jessup, *Painful News*, 161. Some Confederate cavalry regiments were disbanded during the winter; see Longacre, *Lee's Cavalrymen*, 266.
60. Thomas Lupton to "dear father," January 8, 1864, Helena Knight Lupton Collection.
61. Jessup, *Painful News*, 161; Driver and Ruffner, *1st Battalion Virginia Infantry*, 137, 139, 145, 146, 147, 148, 156; Samuel Brown, CMSR.
62. W.W. Page and John J. Jackson, CMSR; John Jackson to R.E. Lee, April 6, 1864, Confederate States of America. Letters Received by the Confederate Secretary of War, 1861–1865. M437, Roll127, RG109, National Archives. Lee Wallace Jr. writes that Company D was organized on June 26, 1864. This appears to be incorrect. *A Guide to Virginia Military Organization, 1861–1865*, 89.
63. Driver and Ruffner, *1st Battalion Virginia Infantry*, 132, 135, 138, 145, 153; Bunch, *Roster of the Courts-Martial in the Confederate States Army*, 38, 43, 128, 199, 211, 272, 340; Albert Pettigrew, CMSR; *Articles of War*, 11; Thomas G. Lupton to "dear father," March 12, 1864, Helena Knight Lupton Collection.
64. *Owensboro Monitor*, March 9, 1864. His Oath of Amnesty, dated March 22, 1864, Washington, D.C., stated Taylor's place of residence was New York City. Holbrook Taylor, CMSR.
65. These numbers were compiled by analyzing the roster in Driver and Ruffner, *1st Battalion Virginia Infantry*, and the compiled military service records; *Richmond Examiner*, March 26, 1864. Thomas G. Lupton wrote that "Johnny" was detailed as an apothecary. It is unclear just who this is. Thomas Lupton to "Dear Sis," March 12, 1864, Helena Knight Lupton Collection.
66. Walter, diary, February 2–29, 1864; Thomas Lupton to "father," March 7, 1864, Helena Knight Lupton Collection.
67. Walter, diary, March 1–April 4, 1864; Walter to "Dear Mother," March 3, 1864, Walter papers.
68. George W. Koiner to sister, March 20, 1864, quoted in Driver and Ruffner, *1st Battalion Virginia Infantry*, 66.
69. Venable, "General Lee in the Wilderness," 240; Walter, diary, April 5–May 5, 1864; Boteler, diary, May 5, 1864, Brooks Collection; Johnson, *In the Footsteps of Robert E. Lee*, 19.
70. C.C. Taliaferro to John W. Daniel, January 7, 1907, John W. Daniel Papers.
71. Ibid.

72. Ibid.

73. Northrop, *Diary of a Prisoner*, 33; Racine, *Unspoiled Heart*, 138–139.

74. Hadley, *Life of Walter Harriman*, 178.

75. Walter, diary, May 7, 1864, May 10, 1864.

76. Taliaferro to Walter Taylor, April 10, 1898, Taylor Papers, Norfolk Public Library; Jones, *Campbell Brown's Civil War*, 251. Taliaferro seems to confuse the events, writing that they took place on both May 10 and 12. Gordon Rhea writes that Taylor had two horses shot from under him on May 10. See *The Battles for Spotsylvania Court House*, 172.

77. Jones, *Campbell Brown's Civil War*, 253.

78. Walter, diary, May 20, 1864.

79. Walter, diary, May 21, 1864; Ferguson, *Life Struggles in Rebel Prisons*, 28–29.

80. Walter, diary, May 24, 1864.

81. Thomas G. Lupton to "sister," May 23, 1864, Helena Knight Lupton Collection.

82. Freeman, R.E. Lee, 3:363; Walter, diary, May 26–30, 1864; Driver and Ruffner, *1st Battalion Virginia Infantry*, 149; Brown CMSR; Page, CMSR.

83. Tower, *Lee's Adjutant*, 165; Thomas Lupton to "Dear Sis," June 4, 1864, Helena Knight Lupton Collection.

84. Thomas G. Lupton to "Dear Sis," June 4, 1864, Helena Knight Lupton Collection.

85. Walter, diary, June 7, 1864.

86. Hagood, *Memoirs of the War of Secession*, 304.

87. Walter, diary, June 11, June 13, June 16, 1864; *Richmond Examiner*, June 13, 1865.

88. Taylor, *General Lee*, 254.

89. Walter, diary, June 18, 1864; Thomas Lupton to "Dear Sister," June 22, 1864, Helena Knight Lupton Collection; Driver and Ruffner, *1st Battalion Virginia Infantry*, 132, 134, 146, 149; Samuel Brown, CMSR.

90. Jessup, *Painful News*, 164; Driver and Ruffner, *1st Battalion Virginia Infantry*, 134, 138, 144; Douglas, *I Rode with Stonewall*, 301.

91. H.J. Cooper to "Dear Miss," July 17, 1864, private collection.

92. Walter, diary, July 9, July 24, July 30, 1864.

93. Driver and Ruffner, *1st Battalion Virginia Infantry*, 148, 149; Samuel B. Brown, CMSR.

94. Tower, *Lee's Adjutant*, 111; Driver and Ruffner, *1st Battalion Virginia Infantry*, 145.

95. Driver and Ruffner, *1st Battalion Virginia Infantry*, 132, 142, 147,148, 149; Charles H. Forsyth, CMSR.

96. George Balthorpe, CMSR; Driver and Ruffner, *1st Battalion Virginia Infantry*, 131, 158.

97. George M. Coiner to "Dear Sister," September 14, 1864, Coiner Letters, quoted in Driver and Ruffner, *1st Battalion Virginia Infantry*, 75; Franklin Walter to "Dear Mother," September 7, 1864, Walter papers.

98. Walter, diary, September 26, October 3, October 10, 1864; Bartholomees, *Buff Facings and Gilt Buttons*, 113–122.

99. Thomas Turner, CMSR; Driver and Ruffner, *1st Battalion Virginia Infantry*, 132, 146, 147, 155, 157.

100. Jessup, *Painful News*, 172–173, 174.

101. Walter, diary, November 1, 1864; Taylor, *Four Years with General Lee*, 141; Coiner letter, November 25, 1864, quoted in Driver and Ruffner, *1st Battalion Virginia Infantry*, 76.

102. Walter, diary, November 1, 1864; Taylor, *Four Years with General Lee*, 142.

103. Jessup, *Painful News*, 177; Coiner letter, November 25, 1864, quoted in Driver and Ruffner, *1st Battalion Virginia Infantry*, 76.

Chapter 4: 1865

104. George Coiner to "Dear Sister," January 2, January 18, 1865, Coiner letters, quoted in Driver and Ruffner, *1st Battalion Virginia Infantry*, 76.

105. Driver and Ruffner, *1st Battalion Virginia Infantry*, 146.

106. Ibid., 151; Bunch, *Roster of the Courts-Martial*, 321.

107. William Ray and James Lupton, CMSR.

108. James H. Warner, CMSR.

109. Driver and Ruffner, *1st Battalion Virginia Infantry*, 148, 149, 150.

110. Freeman, *Lee's Dispatches*, 345; Harrison, *Pickett's Men: A Fragment of War History*, 138; *Confederate Veteran*, 31, 7 (1923): 265.

111. *National Tribune*, July 30, 1908.

112. Hardy, *General Lee's Immortals*, 341.

113. *National Tribune*, July 30, 1908.

114. Walter, diary, April 3, 1865.

115. Driver and Ruffner, *1st Battalion Virginia Infantry*, 153; Walter, diary, April 3–6, 1865.

116. Walter, diary, April 7–8, 1865.

117. Long, *Memoirs of Robert E. Lee*, 420.

118. *Coffeyville Weekly Journal*, March 11, 1876.

119. *Times*, May 15, 1925.

120. Forsyth, "The Closing Scene at Appomattox Court House," 708, 710. For further confirmation that it was indeed Johns at the McLean house, see *New York Daily Herald*, April 14, 1865. See also Marvel, *A Place Called Appomattox*, 351, note 34.

121. *Lenoir Topic*, May 28, 1912. Much of Taliaferro's account was incorrect. He was never a major or a colonel, as articles claimed. Lee had been inside for half an hour prior to Grant's arrival, and Lee left first. There are many mentions of Grant sending rations, but no mentions of tents.

122. Ranson, "General Lee as I Knew Him," 335; Colston, "Recollections of the Last Months," 12.

123. Driver and Ruffner, *1st Battalion Virginia Infantry*, 78.

124. Joshua Passano, CMSR.

125. In 2018, Heritage Auctions placed a copy of General Order No. 9 up for sale. This copy came from Brown's family. Allen, *Down in Dixie*, 462.

126. Driver and Ruffner, *1st Battalion Virginia Infantry*, 134; *Evening Star*, June 23, 1883. Others claimed to have received pieces of the flag. At least four pieces of Lee's headquarters flag are at the American Civil War Museum. See Stewart, *A Pair of Blankets*, 209.

127. These statistics are compiled from the compiled service records of the Thirty-Ninth Battalion Virginia Cavalry and from Driver and Ruffner, *1st Battalion Virginia Infantry*.

128. These statistics are compiled from the compiled service records of the Thirty-Ninth Battalion Virginia Cavalry and from Driver and Ruffner, *1st Battalion Virginia Infantry*.

In Retrospect

129. Bartholomees, *Buff Facings and Gilt Buttons*, 205; Douglas, *I Rode with Stonewall*, 162; Jones, *Campbell Brown's Civil War*, 197.

130. Driver and Ruffner, *1st Battalion Virginia Infantry*, 142, 143, 154, 156.

131. Sorrel, *Recollections*, 259. E. Porter Alexander makes mention of a similar event, stating one of the couriers was killed. Gallagher, *Fighting for the Confederacy*, 389.

132. Thirty-Ninth Battalion folder, Library of Virginia; John N. Opie, CMSR; Opie, *A Rebel Cavalryman*.

133. *Alexandria Gazette*, October 6, 1892; *Illustrated Monthly Magazine*, April 1891, vol. 61, 19: 797–1,098; *New York Times*, February 26, 1878; *Baltimore Sun*, July 4, 1913.

134. Randolph's compiled service record states he was captured in Fauquier County on September 9, 1863. However, there are no Federal records to corroborate this. William F. Randolph, CMSR; *Biographical and Historical Memoirs of Mississippi*, 2: 638–639; *Alexander Gazette*, August 1, 1914; *New York Tribune*, August 1, 1914; *Cincinnati Enquirer*, August 1, 1914.

135. Driver and Ruffner, *1st Battalion Virginia Infantry*, 149; *Newberry Weekly Herald*, May 21, 1907.

136. *Times*, November 30, 1900; Allardice, *Confederate Colonels*, 323.

137. Driver and Ruffner, *1st Battalion Virginia Infantry*, 132; *Confederate Veteran* (September 1920), vol. 28, no. 9, 347; "Confederate Veteran Camp of New York," 455; *Illustrated Monthly Magazine*, April 1891, vol. 61, 19: 797–1,098; *New York Herald*, June 15, 1920.

138. *Cumberland Evening Times*, July 23, 1930; *News Leader*, June 3, 1918; *Evening Sun*, April 12, 1923.

139. *New Orleans States*, April 28, 1922; *Richmond Dispatch*, March 2, 1902; *Washington Times*, August 21, 1921; *News Leader*, October 10, 1921; *Free Lance*, January 19, 1904; *Atlanta Constitution*, November 9, 1926.

140. *Topeka Daily Capital*, October 2, 1885.

141. *Manassas Journal*, August 27, 1931.

BIBLIOGRAPHY

Unpublished Manuscripts

Handley Library
  —Helena Knight Lupton Collection
Library of Congress
  —William E. Brooks Collection
  —Alexander Boteler Diary
Library of Virginia
  —Virginia Department of Confederate Military Records
National Archives
  —Compiled Military Service Records of Confederate Soldiers Who Served in Organizations from the State of Virginia, Microfilm No. M324, Rolls 197–199
  —Letters Received by the Confederate Secretary of War, 1861–1865. M437
Norfolk Public Library
  —Colonel Walter H. Taylor Papers, Sargeant Memorial Collection
Private collection in possession of the author
  —Henry Jackson Cooper letters
University of Virginia
  —John Warwick Daniel Papers

Newspapers and Magazines

Alexander Gazette (Virginia)
Asheville Citizen-Times (North Carolina)
Atlanta Constitution (Georgia)
Baltimore Sun (Maryland)
Birmingham Daily Post (England)
Cincinnati Enquirer (Ohio)
Coffeyville Weekly (Kansas)
Confederate Veteran
Cumberland Evening Times (Maryland)
Free Lance (Fredericksburg, Virginia)
Harper's Weekly
Land We Love
Lenoir Topic (North Carolina)
Manassas Journal (Virginia)
National Tribune (Washington, D.C.)
Newberry Weekly Herald (South Carolina)
New Orleans States (Louisiana)
News Leader (Virginia)
New York Daily Herald
New York Times
New York Tribune
Owensboro Monitor (Kentucky)
Richmond Dispatch (Virginia)
Richmond Examiner (Virginia)
Sentinel (Virginia)
Topeka Daily Capital (Kansas)
Washington Times (Washington, D.C.)

Published Sources

Allardice, Bruce S. *Confederate Colonels: A Biographical Register.* Columbia: University of Missouri Press, 2008.

Allen, Stanton P. *Down in Dixie: Life in a Cavalry Regiment in the War Days.* Boston: D. Lothrop Co., 1893.

Articles of War for the Government of the Confederate States of America. Montgomery, AL: Barrett, Wimbish, & Co., 1861.

Bartholomees, J. Boone, Jr. *Buff Facings and Gilt Buttons.* Columbia: University of South Carolina Press, 1998.

Bigelow, John. *The Campaign of Chancellorsville.* New Haven, CT: Yale University Press, 1910.

Biographical and Historical Memoirs of Mississippi. 2 vols. Chicago: The Goodspeed Publishing Company, 1891.

Bunch, Jack A. *Roster of the Courts-Martial in the Confederate States Army.* Shippensburg, PA: White Mane Publishing Co, Inc., 2001.

Burns, Brian. *Curiosities of the Confederate Capital.* Charleston, SC: The History Press, 2013.

Cartmell, T.K. *Shenandoah Valley Pioneers and Their Descendants.* N.p., 1909.

Clark, Walter. *Histories of the Several Regiments and Battalions from North Carolina in the Great War 1861–'65.* 5 vols. Raleigh, NC: E.M. Uzzell, Printer and Binder, 1901.

Colston, Frederick M. "Recollections of the Last Months in the Army of Northern Virginia." *Southern Historical Society Papers.* Vol. 38. (January–December 1910): 1–15.

"Confederate Veteran Camp of New York." *The National Magazine,* August 1892: 455–480.

Douglas, Henry K. *I Rode with Stonewall.* Chapel Hill: University of North Carolina Press, 1940.

Dowdey, Clifford. *Lee's Last Campaign: The Story of Lee and His Men Against Grant–1864.* Boston: Random House, 1960.

Driver, Robert J., Jr., and Kevin C. Ruffner. *1st Battalion Virginia Infantry, 39th Battalion Virginia Cavalry, 24th Battalion Virginia Partisan Rangers.* Lynchburg, VA: H.E. Howard, [1996].

Ewell, Alice M. *Virginia Scenes or Life in Old Prince William.* Lynchburg, VA: J.P. Bell, 1931.

Ferguson, Joseph. *Life Struggles in Rebel Prisons.* Philadelphia: James M. Ferguson Publishing, 1865.

Forsyth, George A. "The Closing Scene at Appomattox Court House." *Harper's Magazine,* 96, no. 575: 700–11.

Freeman, Douglas S. *Lee's Dispatches.* New York: G.P. Putnam's Sons, 1915.

———. *R.E. Lee: A Biography.* 4 vols. New York: Charles Scribner's Sons, 1934–1935.

Gallagher, Gary W., ed. *Fighting for the Confederacy: The Personal Recollections of General Edward Porter Alexander.* Chapel Hill: University of North Carolina Press, 1989.

Greene, Katherine G. *Stony Mead: A Sketch*. Strasburg, VA: Shenandoah Publishing House, Inc., 1929.

Hadley, Amos. *Life of Walter Harriman*. Boston: Houghton, Mifflin and Company, 1888.

Hagood, Johnson. *Memoirs of the War of Secession*. Columbia, SC: The State Company, 1910.

Hardy, Michael C. *General Lee's Immortals: The Battles and Campaigns of the Branch-Lane Brigade in the Army of Northern Virginia*. El Dorado Hills, CA: Savas Beatie, 2018.

Harrison, Walter. *Pickett's Men: A Fragment of War History*. New York: D. Van Nostand, Publisher, 1870.

Hewett, Janet. *Supplement to the Official Records of the Union and Confederate Armies*. 100 vols. Wilmington, NC: Broadfoot Publishing Company, 1994–2001.

Jessup, Harlan R. *The Painful News I Have to Write*. Baltimore, MD: Butternut and Blue, 1998.

Johnson, Clint. *In the Footsteps of Robert E. Lee*. Winston-Salem, NC: John F. Blair, 2001.

Johnson, Robert U., and Clarence C. Buel, eds. *Battles and Leaders of the Civil War*. 4 vols. New York: The Century Company, 1888.

Jones, Terry L., ed. *Campbell Brown's Civil War: With Ewell and the Army of Northern Virginia*. Baton Rouge: Louisiana State University Press, 2001.

Keen, Hugh C., and Horace Mewborn. *43rd Battalion Virginia Cavalry Mosby's Command*. Lynchburg, VA: H.E. Howard, 1993.

Krick, Robert K. *The Smoothbore Valley that Doomed the Confederacy*. Baton Rouge: Louisiana State University Press, 2002.

Lee, Wallace A. *A Guide to Virginia Military Organizations, 1861–1865*. Lynchburg, VA: H.E. Howard, 1986.

Long, A.L. *Memoirs of Robert E. Lee*. New York: 1886.

Longacre, Edward G. *Lee's Cavalrymen: A History of the Mounted Forces of the Army of Northern Virginia*. Mechanicsville, PA: Stackpole Books, 2002.

Marvel, William. *A Place Called Appomattox*. Chapel Hill: The University of North Carolina Press, 2008.

Maurice, Frederick. *An Aide-de-Camp of Lee*. Boston: Little, Brown and Company, 1927.

Myers, Frank M. *The Comanches: A History of White's Battalion, Virginia Cavalry*. Baltimore, MD: Kelly, Piet & Co., 1871.

Northrop, John. *Chronicles from the Diary of a Prisoner in Andersonville*. Wichita, KS: John Northrop, 1904.

Opie, John N. *A Rebel Cavalryman with Lee, Stuart and Jackson.* Chicago: W.B. Conkey Co., 1899.

Pfanz, Donald. *The Letters of Richard S. Ewell: Stonewall's Successor.* Knoxville: University of Tennessee Press, 2012.

———. *Richard S. Ewell.* Chapel Hill: University of North Carolina Press, 1998.

Racine, Philip N., ed. *Unspoiled Heart: The Journal of Charles Mattocks of the 17th Maine.* Knoxville: University of Tennessee Press, 1994.

Randolph, William F. "With Stonewall Jackson at Chancellorsville," *Southern Churchman*, April 11, 1931.

Ranson, A.R.H. "General Lee as I Knew Him." *Harper's Magazine* (February 1911), 122, no. 729: 327–36.

Regulations for the Army of the Confederate States, 1863. Richmond: J.W. Randolph, 1863.

Rhea, Gordon C. *The Battle for Spotsylvania Court House and the Road to Yellow Tavern, May 7–12, 1864.* Baton Rouge: Louisiana State University Press, 1997.

Robertson, James I. *Stonewall Jackson: The Man, the Soldier, the Legend.* New York: Macmillan Publishing, 1997.

Smith, Timothy H. *The Story of Lee's Headquarters.* Gettysburg, PA: Thomas Publications, 1995.

Sorrel, G. Moxley. *Recollections of a Confederate Staff Officer.* New York: Neal Publishing Company, 1905.

Stewart, William H. *A Pair of Blankets.* New York: Broadway Publishing Co., 1911.

Swank, Walbrook D. *Courier for Lee and Jackson.* Shippensburg, PA: White Mane Publishing Co, Inc., 1993.

Taylor, Walter H. *Four Years with General Lee.* New York: D. Appleton and Company, 1878.

———. *General Lee: His Campaigns in Virginia, 1861–1865.* Norfolk, VA: Nusbaum Book and News Company, 1906.

Tower, R. Lockwood, ed. *Lee's Adjutant: The Wartime Letters of Colonel Walter Herron Taylor, 1862–1864.* Columbia: University of South Carolina Press, 1995.

Venable, Charles S. "General Lee in the Wilderness Campaign." *Battles and Leaders of the Civil War.* Vol. 4 : 240–46. New York: The Century Co., 1888.

The War of the Rebellion: A Compilation of the Official Records of the Union and Confederate Armies, 128 vols. Washington, D.C.: 1880–1901.

Wiley, Bell I., ed. *Reminiscences of Confederate Service, 1861–1865 Francis W. Dawson.* Baton Rouge: Louisiana State University Press, 1980.

Index

ABOUT THE AUTHOR

Michael C. Hardy's interest in Confederate regimentals goes back over three decades. Of the twenty-four books he has written, four have concerned regiments or brigades. One reviewer attests: "Michael Hardy demonstrates an in-depth knowledge of the inner workings of Civil War units." Some of his other books chronicle specific battles, while others recount the history of particular locations. Michael's articles have appeared in numerous publications, and he has posted over one thousand times on his blog, *Looking for the Confederate War*.

Michael has called western North Carolina home since 1995. He is a graduate of the University of Alabama, and in 2010, he was named North Carolina's Historian of the Year by the North Carolina Society of Historians. Michael has appeared in *Blood and Fury* on the American Heroes Channel and on *Civil War Talk Radio*. He spends many of his weekends volunteering at historic sites as an interpreter working to help people understand the past.

Visit us at
www.historypress.com